Blackfeet Tales of Glacier National Park

BY
JAMES WILLARD SCHULTZ

With Illustrations

T0163493

RIVERBEND
PUBLISHING

Cover Photo: Blackfeet at Ptarmigan Falls, Glacier National Park.
Montana Historical Society, Helena.

Copyright © 1916 by James Willard Schultz

Original elements of this edition copyright © 2002
by Riverbend Publishing.

Published by Riverbend Publishing, Helena, Montana.

Printed in the United States of America.

12 13 14 MG

All rights reserved. No part of this book may be reproduced, stored, or
transmitted in any form or by any means without the prior permission
of the publisher, with the exception of brief excerpts for reviews.

Cover design by Laurie "gigette" Gould.
Text design by Suzan Glosser.

ISBN 978-1-931832-14-4

Cataloging-in-Publication data is on file at the
Library of Congress.

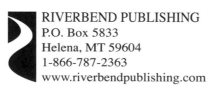

RIVERBEND PUBLISHING
P.O. Box 5833
Helena, MT 59604
1-866-787-2363
www.riverbendpublishing.com

To
Louis Warren Hill, Esq.

TRUE FRIEND TO MY BLACKFEET PEOPLE, AND THE ONE WHO
HAS DONE MORE THAN ANY OTHER INDIVIDUAL, OR ANY
ORGANIZATION, TO MAKE THE WONDERS OF GLACIER NA-
TIONAL PARK ACCESSIBLE TO THE AMERICAN PEOPLE, THIS
BOOK IS DEDICATED BY

THE AUTHOR

GLACIER NATIONAL PARK,
SEPTEMBER 10, 1915.

Contents

INTRODUCTION

BY DARRELL ROBES KIPP

EXECUTIVE DIRECTOR OF THE PIEGAN INSTITUTE
BROWNING, MONTANA

In 1944, a few days after I was born, my grandmother gave me the name, Apiniokio Peta, Morning Eagle, the honored name of her uncle. My grandmother's English name was Mary Kipp, and she was the wife of Sequeenamakah, Last Gun, who appeared in one of James Willard Schultz's books as Makapini, or Red Eyes. A survivor of the infamous Baker Massacre on the Bear River in 1870, Last Gun, whose English name was Richard Kipp, grew up in the household of Joseph Kipp, one of the army scouts involved in the massacre. Perhaps in part to repair his reputation among the Blackfeet tribe, Kipp took in a number of children orphaned in the massacre and later married one of them, Last Gun's sister Double Strike Woman. Joseph Kipp, whom Schultz calls Berry in his books, was one of the first friends Schultz made after arriving in Fort Benton in 1877, and many of Schultz's tales originate from their close association. Certainly, then, my grandfather, who grew up in Kipp's household, knew Schultz well as did my grandmother and their children.

I remember, as a child, listening to my father, Thomas Kipp, tell us his father's stories from the days when Last Gun hauled freight in horse drawn wagons for Joseph Kipp. In the fashion of children listening to their parents' stories, I seldom connected them to the greater story of the tribe, and it was not until years later, when I began to read Schultz's books, did I discover the various connections between our family and Schultz's life among the Blackfeet.

James Willard Shultz came among the Blackfeet in a pivotal period: the end of the buffalo hunting days for all plains tribes, including the Blackfeet, occurred less than ten years after his arrival in Montana. The Blackfeet were people of the buffalo, and much of their life ways derived from their relationship with the buffalo herds. It is safe to say that the tribe faced great disorder and misfortune following the buffalo's demise.

Much has been written about the status of Indians since then, with many chroniclers insisting that "real" Indians ceased to exist once the buffalo hunting days were over. This is a slap in the face to Indians living today, and I among them cringe at such statements. One of the reasons I like Schultz's work is that he never puts Indians away as relics of a past era, but through his storytelling keeps the old days fresh in his reader's mind.

The idea that modern Indians are somehow not "real" Indians continues to exist today. It is, of course, a very ethnocentric viewpoint, and if applied to American society in general would lead to the view that there are no "real" Americans left in this country, for just as Indians' circumstances have changed over the last two hundred years, so have the circumstances of their white counterparts. Among the Blackfeet, introduction of horses, guns, and, for that matter, steel, automobiles, and computers has marked the end of various earlier epochs, but the tribe's bonds have remained strong, as has a continuing appreciation among tribal members for timeless stories about our history, and how our people have adapted to these changes. Today, Indians seek knowledge of their past just like any other group, and Schultz's work serves their purpose well.

My fellow tribal members who enjoy Schultz's books give him high marks for storytelling and for keeping memories alive. While some purists scoff at the way he romanticized our tribal history, most of us rejoice in his recollections. We especially rejoice because he was so prolific, and his stories cover the gamut of the tribe's trials and tribulations, as well as our oral tradition.

Some have criticized Schultz for placing himself in his stories at the expense of objectivity. I would argue, in fact, that this is one of his strengths as a writer. He could put himself into the story as easily as he put the reader into it. While his work doesn't meet academic standards of objectivity, it isn't dry and pedantically academic, either. Others have questioned Schultz's competence in speaking the Blackfeet language. Certainly, however, he communicated well in the language, as well as in sign language, and this is reflected in his writings. (After all, his wife Natahki did not speak English, nor did most of tribal members Schultz knew during the time he lived among them.) This fact alone separates him from most of the other chroniclers of the Blackfeet people: he spoke the language and, through his marriage to Natahki, had access to all their inner sanctum settings, as well daily life trials and tribulation. (It is important to understand that marriage within the tribe was viewed first and foremost as an alliance and marked the taking on of an ally, so Schultz's marriage was viewed, by members of the tribe as a significant connection.)

In addition to having access to tribal stories and rituals, Schultz also had access to white trappers and traders known to the tribe such as James Bird, Charles Rivois, Joe Kipp, and the venerated Hugh Monroe (Rising Wolf). These men were a virtual library of Blackfeet lore, and they, like Schultz, understood the basic rule of Blackfeet storytelling: truth. For among the Blackfeet, the primary element in how they honored the Creator's work derived from truthfulness. A story without truth was considered an insult to the listeners. So, although Schultz sometimes used poetic license in addressing his literary audiences, it was unlikely he could bring himself to roam too far afield without trepidation. Schultz's detractors balk at his sweeping judgments, his inexact and inconsistent chronology, and his renaming of characters, but in all, as a tribal member, I have no reason not to rely on his work as recollections of someone who was there. Other informed tribal members confirm my perspective and praise the authenticity of Schultz's descriptions of various Blackfeet ceremonies.

Schultz's intimacy with the Blackfeet extended to his intimacy with Glacier National Park. As his biographer Warren L. Hanna, states in *The Life and Times of James Willard Schultz (Apikuni)*, "I am satisfied that no one has done more to make the park beloved, as well as famous, than James Willard Schultz." In fact, Schultz helped discover—and promote—many of the park's major attractions, if the word "discover" is used to mean "discover by non-Indians." The oral tradition of the tribe fully chronicles the glaciers, lakes, mountains, streams, and trails of the area with long-established Blackfeet names and descriptions. From these tribal traditions, Schultz undoubtedly had learned a great deal about the area before he actually traveled it with the George Bird Grinnell in 1884. Schultz certainly influenced the naming of various topographical elements in the area, though many of his names echoed names taught to him by the Blackfeet people.

The establishment of the park was the dream of writer and editor of *Forest and Stream* George Bird Grinnell, who viewed it as a scheme worthy of taking up with Louis Hill, president of the Great Northern Railway. Hill helped push Congress to authorize the park in 1910 and then worked hard to promote it as a tourist destination—with the expectation that the tourists would travel there via his railroad. Schultz remained beholden to both Grinnell and Hill because they purchased his writings, and he often made it clear to them he would write what they wanted. These offers have put Schultz's reputation for accuracy in jeopardy, yet the fact that Schultz wrote for mercenary reasons should not necessarily discredit his stories.

Ultimately, Schultz's place among the Blackfeet tribe was one of long-term friend and fellow traveler. His marriage to a Blackfeet woman connected him to the tribe, and the birth of his son, Hart Merriam Schultz, or Lone Wolf, strengthened that connection. In 1985, during my early work as a language researcher among my tribe, there still were individuals who remembered Schultz personally, and their recollections were of a man who lived with them and was accepted as part of the tribe. His burial by the tribe near Two Medicine River is testament to his acceptance and strong alliance.

Academics find it easy to criticize in Schultz for his romanticism, lack of objectivity, and casual scholarship, but in my view his strengths outweigh his flaws. A prolific, excellent storyteller, he presented the essence of the Blackfeet tribe as no other writer was able to then or has since. Schultz's *Blackfeet Tales of Glacier National Park* offers an excellent opportunity for readers to get a full dose of his working style and to get to know Blackfeet traditions and the area now known as Glacier National Park. I am pleased to see this book back in print, and I hope it draws a new audience to other books by this remarkable writer.

Blackfeet Tales of Glacier National Park

I

TWO MEDICINE

HUGH MONROE

July 12, 1915.

AFTER an absence of many years, I have returned to visit for a time my Blackfeet relatives and friends, and we are camping along the mountain trails where, in the long ago, we hunted buffalo, and elk, and moose, and all the other game peculiar to this region.

To-day we pitched our lodges under Rising Wolf Mountain, that massive, sky-piercing, snow-crested height of red-and-gray rock which slopes up so steeply from the north shore of Upper Two Medicine Lake. This afternoon we saw upon it, some two or three thousand feet up toward its rugged crest, a few bighorn and a Rocky Mountain goat. But we may not kill them! Said Tail-Feathers-Coming-over-the-Hill: "There they are! Our meat, but the whites have taken them from us, even as they have taken everything else that is ours!" And so we are eating beef where once we feasted upon the rich ribs and loins of game, which tasted all the better because we trailed and killed it, and with no little labor brought it to the womenfolk in camp.

Rising Wolf Mountain! What a fitting and splendid monument it is to the first white man to traverse the foothills of the Rockies between the Saskatchewan and the Missouri! Hugh Monroe was his English name. His father was Captain Hugh Monroe, of the English army; his mother was Amélie de la Roche, a daughter of a noble family of French *émigrés*. Hugh Monroe, junior, was born in Montreal in 1798. In 1814 he received permission to enter the employ of the Hudson's Bay Company, and one year later — in the summer of 1815 — he arrived at its new post, Mountain Fort, on the North Fork of the Saskatchewan and close to the foot-hills of the Rockies.

At that time the Company had but recently entered Blackfeet territory, and none of its *engagés* understood their language; an interpreter was needed, and the Factor appointed Monroe to fit himself for the position. The Blackfeet

Hugh Monroe

were leaving the Fort to hunt and trap along the tributaries of the Missouri during the winter, and he went with them, under the protection of the head chief, who had nineteen wives and two lodges and an immense band of horses. By easy stages they traveled along the foot of the Rockies to Sun River, where they wintered, and then in the spring, instead of returning to the Saskatchewan, they crossed the Missouri, hunted in the Yellowstone country that summer, wintered on the Missouri at the mouth of the Marias River, and returned to Mountain Fort the following spring with all the furs their horses could carry.

Instead of one winter, Monroe had passed two years with the tribe, and in that time had acquired a wife, a daughter of the great chief, a good knowledge of the language, and an honorable name, Ma-kwi´-i-po-wak-sin (Rising Wolf), which was given him because of his bravery in a battle with the Crows in the Yellowstone country.

During Monroe's two years' absence from the Fort, another *engagé* had learned the Blackfeet language from a Cree Indian, who spoke it well, so that this man became the interpreter, and Monroe was ordered to remain with the Piegan tribe of the Blackfeet, to travel with them, and

3

see that they came annually to the Fort to trade in the winter catch of furs. And this exactly suited him; he much preferred roaming the plains with his chosen people; the stuffy rooms of the Fort had no attractions for a man of his nature.

How I envy Hugh Monroe, the first white man to traverse the plains lying between the Upper Saskatchewan and the Upper Missouri, and the first to see many portions of the great stretch of the mountain region between the Missouri and the Yellowstone. He has himself often told me that "every day of that life was a day of great joy!"

Monroe was a famous hunter and trapper, and a warrior as well. He was a member of the Ai´-in-i-kiks, or Seizer band of the All Friends Society, and the duty of the Seizers was to keep order in the great camp, and see that the people obeyed hunting laws—a most difficult task at times. On several occasions he went with his and other bands to war against other tribes, and once, near Great Salt Lake, when with a party of nearly two hundred warriors, he saved the lives of the noted Jim Bridger and his party of trappers. Bridger had with him a dozen white men and as many Snake Indians, the latter bitter enemies of the Blackfeet. The Snakes were discovered, and the Blackfeet party was preparing to charge them, when Monroe saw that there were white men behind them. "Stop! White men are with them! We must let them go their way in peace!" Monroe shouted to his party.

"But they are Snake white men, and therefore our enemy: we shall kill them all!" the Blackfeet chief answered. However, such was Monroe's power over his comrades that he finally persuaded them to remain where they were, and he went forward with a flag of truce, and found that his friend Jim Bridger was the leader of the other party. That evening white men and Snakes and Blackfeet ate and smoked together! It was a narrow escape for Bridger and his handful of men.

Monroe had three sons and three daughters by his Indian wife, all of whom grew into fine, stalwart men and women. Up and down the country he roamed with them, trapping and hunting, and often fighting hostile war parties. They finally all married, and in his old age he lived with one and another of them until his death, in 1896, in his ninety-eighth year. We buried him near the buffalo cliffs, down on the Two Medicine River, where he had seen many a herd of the huge animals decoyed to their death. And then we named this mountain for him. A fitting tribute, I think, to one of the bravest yet most kindly men of the old, old West!

At the upper east side and head of this beautiful lake rises a pyramidal mountain of great height and grandeur. A frowse of pine timber on its lower front slope, and its ever-narrowing side slopes above, give it a certain resemblance to a buffalo bull. Upon looking at a recent map of the country I found that it had been named "Mount Rockwell." So, turning to Yellow Wolf, I said: "The whites have given that mountain yonder the name of a white man. It is so marked upon this paper."

The old man, half blind and quite feeble, roused up when he heard that, and cried out: "Is it so? Not satisfied with taking our mountains, the whites even take away the ancient names we have given them! They shall not do it! You tell them so! That mountain yonder is Rising Bull Mountain, and by that name it must ever be called! Rising Bull was one of our

Rising Bull

great chiefs: what more fitting than that the mountain should always bear his name?"

"Rising Bull was a chief in two tribes," Yellow Wolf went on. "In his youth he married a Flathead girl, at a time when we were at peace with that people, and after a winter or two she persuaded him to take her across the mountains for a visit with her relatives. Rising Bull came to like them and all the Flathead people so well that he remained with them a number of winters, and because of his bravery, and his kind and generous nature, the Flatheads soon appointed him one of their chiefs. When he was about forty winters of age, some young men of both tribes quarreled over a gambling game and several were killed on each side. That, of course, ended the peace pact; war was declared, and as Rising Bull could not fight his own people, he came back to us with his Flathead wife, and was a leader in the war, which lasted for several years. When that was ended, he continued to lead war parties against the Crows, the Sioux, the Assiniboines, and the far-off Snakes, and was always successful. Came the dreadful Measles Winter,[1] and with hundreds of our people, he died. He left a son, White Quiver, a very brave

[1] The winter of 1859-60.

young warrior, and two years after his father's death, he was killed in a raid against the Crows.

"Ai! Rising Bull was a brave man. And oh, so gentle-hearted! So good to the widows and orphans; to all in any kind of distress! We must in some way see that this mountain continues to bear his name," said Tail-Feathers-Coming-over-the-Hill.

And to that I most heartily agree.

July 15.

We are a considerable camp of people: Yellow Wolf, my old uncle-in-law; Tail-Feathers-Coming-over-the-Hill, another uncle-in-law; Big Spring; Two Guns; Black Bull; Stabs-by-Mistake; Eagle Child; Eli Guardipe, or Takes-Gun-Ahead. And with them they have their eleven women and fourteen children. All are my especial friends, and all the men have been to war — some of them many times — and have counted cup upon the enemy. Tail-Feathers-Coming over-the-Hill has many battle scars on different parts of his body. I was with him when he got the last one, in a fight with the Crees. The bullet struck him in the forehead, ripped open the scalp clear to the back of his head, but did not penetrate the skull. He dropped instantly when struck, and we at first thought that he was dead. It was some hours before he regained consciousness.

With all these men, and especially Tail-Feathers-Coming-over-the-Hill and Guardipe, I hunted and traveled much in the old days. Naturally, we spend much of our time telling over this-and-that of our adventures. Meantime the children play around, as happy as Indian children ever are, and their mothers do the lodge work, which is light, and gather in groups to chat and joke. The boys have just been skipping stones on the smooth surface of the lake. The number of skips a stone makes before it finally sinks, denotes the number of wives the caster will have when he reaches manhood.

Tail-Feathers-Coming-over-the-Hill and Two Guns are medicine men. The former has the Elk medicine pipe, the latter the Water medicine pipe, both ancient medicines in the tribe. They are spiritual, not material, medicines. In fact, they are the implements used in prayers to the sun and other gods, and each carries with it

Blackfeet Tales of Glacier National Park

a ritual of its own. Tail-Feathers-Coming-over the-Hill has just told me that we will have some prayers with his pipe a few days from now. I shall be glad to take part in it all once more.

Again my people are filled with resentment against the whites. I told them this afternoon that the falls in the river between this and the lower lake had been given a foolish white men's name. I could not tell them what it was, for there is no Blackfeet equivalent for the word "Trick." But what a miserable, circus-suggesting name that is to give to one of the most beautiful of waterfalls, and the only one of its kind in America, and in all the world, for all I know! A short distance below the outlet of the upper lake the river sinks; and a half-mile farther on gushes into sight from a jagged hole halfway up the side of a high and almost perpendicular cliff.

"In the long ago we named that Pi´tamakan Falls," said Tail-Feathers-Coming-over-the-Hill. "Yes? And who was he?" I asked, although I had a fair recollection of the story of that personage. But I had forgotten the details of it, and wanted them all.

"Not he, but she!" he corrected me.

10

The Story of Running Eagle

"But Pi´tamakan (Running Eagle) is a man's name," I objected.

"True. But this woman earned the right to bear a man's name, and so it was given her. She was the only woman of our people to receive that honor, so far as I know. Listen! You shall hear all about it.

THE WOMAN WHO EARNED A MAN'S NAME

"As a girl, her name was Weasel Woman. She was the eldest of two brothers and two sisters, and when she had seen fifteen winters both their father and mother died. But unlike children in such circumstances, they did not give up their lodge and scatter out to live with relatives and friends. Said Weasel Woman: 'Somehow, some way, we can manage to live. You boys are old enough to hunt and bring in meat and skins. We three sisters will keep the lodge in good order, and tan the skins for our clothing and bedding, and other uses.' And as she said, so it was done, and the orphan family prospered.

"But Weasel Woman was not satisfied. Many young men and many old and rich men wanted to marry her, and to all she said 'No !' so loudly, and so quickly, that after a time all knew that

11

she would not marry. Wherever a party of warriors gathered for a dance or a feast, there she was looking on, listening to their talk, and giving what help she could. And when a party returned from war, she was loudest in praising them. All she talked of, all she thought about, was war.

"On an evening in her twentieth summer a large party of warriors started out to cross the mountains and raid the Flatheads. They traveled all night, and when daylight came found that Weasel Woman was with them.

"'Go back! Go home!' the war chief told her. But she would not listen.

"'If you will not let me go with you, I shall follow you,' she said.

And then spoke up the medicine man of the party: 'Chief,' said he, 'I advise you to allow her to go with us; something tells me that she will bring us good luck.'

"'Ah! As you advise me, so shall it be,' said the war chief; and the woman went on with them. No man of that party teased her, nor bothered her in any way: every one of them treated her as they would a sister. It was the strangest war party that ever set forth from any tribe of the plains!

The Story of Running Eagle

" 'It was at the edge of Flathead Lake that they discovered the enemy, a large camp of the Flatheads and their friends, the Pend d'Oreilles. When night came they went close up to it, and the woman said to the war chief: 'Let me go in first. Let me see what I can do. I feel that I shall be successful in there.'

" 'Go!' the chief told her, 'and we will wait for you here, and be ready to help you if you get into trouble.'

"The woman went into the camp, where all the best horses of the people — their fast buffalo runners, their racers, and their stallions — were picketed close to the lodges of the different owners of them. If she was afraid of being discovered and killed, she never admitted it. The dying moon gave light enough for her to see the size and color of the horses. She took her time and went around among them, and, making her choice, cut the ropes of three fine pinto horses, and led them out to where the party awaited her. There she tied them, and went back into camp with the chief and his men and again came out with three horses. Said she then: 'I have taken enough for this time. I will await you here and take care of what we have.'

Blackfeet Tales of Glacier National Park

"The men went back several times, and then, having all the horses that they could drive rapidly, the party struck for the mountains, and in several days' time arrived home without the loss of a man or a horse.

"A few days after the party came into camp the medicine lodge was put up, and on the day that the warriors counted their *coups*, and new names were given them, an old warrior and medicine man called Weasel Woman before the people, and had her count her *coup* — of going twice into the enemy's camp and taking six horses. All shouted approval of that, and then the medicine man gave her the name, Pi′-ta-mak-an, a very great one, that of a chief whose shadow had some time before gone on to the Sand Hills.

"After that Pi′tamakan, as we now may call her, did not have to sneak after a party in order to go to war with them: she was asked to go. And after two or three more successful raids against different enemies, the Crows, the Sioux, and the Flatheads, she herself became a war chief, and warriors begged to be allowed to join her parties, because they believed that where she led nothing but good luck would come to them. She now wore men's clothing when on a raid.

The Story of Running Eagle

At home she wore her woman clothing. But even in that dress she, like any man, gave feasts and dances, and the greatest chiefs and warriors came to them, and were glad to be there.

"On her sixth raid, Pi´tamakan led a large war party against the Flatheads, and somewhere on the other side of the mountains fell in with a war party of Bloods, one of our brother tribes of the North. For several days the two parties traveled along together, and then one evening the Blood chief, Falling Bear, said to Pi´tamakan's servant: 'Go tell your chief woman that I would like to marry her.'

"'Chief, you do not understand,' the boy told him. 'She is not that kind. Men are her brothers, and nothing more. She will never marry. I cannot give her your message, for I am afraid that she would be angry with me for carrying it to her.'

"On the next day, as they were traveling on, the Blood chief said to Pi´tamakan: 'I have never loved, but I love now. I love you; my heart is all yours; let us marry.'

"'I will not say "yes" to that, nor will I say "no,"' the woman chief answered him. 'I will consider what you ask, and give you an answer after we make this raid.'

"And with that the Blood chief said no more, but felt encouraged: he thought that in time she would agree to become his woman.

"That very evening the scouts ahead discovered a large camp of Flathead and Kootenai Indians, more than a hundred lodges of them, and when night came both parties drew close in to it. Pi´tamakan then ordered her followers to remain where they were and told the Blood chief to say the same thing to his men. She then told the Blood chief to go into the camp and take horses, and he went in and returned with one horse.

"'It is now my turn,' said Pi´tamakan, and she went in and brought out two horses.

"The Blood chief went in and brought out two horses.

"Pi´tamakan went in and brought out four horses.

"The Blood chief went in and brought out two horses.

"Pi´tamakan went in and brought out one horse. And then she said to the Blood chief: 'Our men are becoming impatient to go in there and take horses. We will each of us go in once more, and then let them do what they can.'

"So the Blood chief went in for the fourth and last time, and came back leading four horses, making nine in all. And then Pi´tamakan went in and cut the ropes of eight horses, and safely led them out, making in all fifteen that she had taken. The warriors then went in, making several trips, and then, with all the horses that could be easily driven, the big double party headed for home.

"On the next day, as Pi´tamakan and the Blood chief were riding together, he said to her: 'I love you so much that I can wait no longer for my answer. Give it to me now. I believe that you are going to say, "Yes, I will be your woman." '

Said Pi´tamakan: 'I gave you your chance. It would have been yes had you taken more horses than I did from the camp of the enemy. But I took the most; therefore I cannot marry you.'

"That was her way of getting around saying 'no' to the chief. She had beaten him, an old, experienced warrior, in the taking of the enemy's horses, and he could not ask her again to become his woman. It is said that he felt very badly about it all.

Blackfeet Tales of Glacier National Park

"Pi´tamakan now carried a gun when she went to war, and used it well in several fights with the enemy, counting in all three *coups*, each one of them the taking of a gun from the man she herself killed. And then, *haiya*! On her ninth raid she led a party against the Flatheads, and while she and all her men were in the camp, choosing horses and cutting their ropes, the Flatheads discovered them and began firing, and she and five of her men were killed. And so passed Pi´tamakan, virgin, and brave woman chief of our people. She died young, about seventy winters ago."

Okan, his vision, is the name the Blackfeet have for the great lodge which they annually give to the sun, and for the four days of ceremonies attending its erection and consecration. In our vernacular it is the medicine lodge. I asked Yellow Wolf this afternnon why this river was name Nat´-ok-i-o-kan, or, as we say, Two Medicine Lodge River, and he replied that when the Blackfeet first took this great country from the Crows, they built a medicine lodge on the river, just below the buffalo cliffs. The next summer they built another one in the same place, and owing to that the river got its name.

AT UPPER TWO MEDICINE LAKE

Left to right:Tail-feathers-coming-over-the-hill, Yellow Wolf, and the author, relating his
killing of a grizzly at this particular place, in the long-ago

Blackfeet Tales of Glacier National Park

Yes, this was once the country of the Crows. But the Blackfeet saw and coveted it. It was about two hundred years ago, as near as I can learn, that they came into it from their original home, the region of Peace River and the Slave Lakes, and little by little forced the Crows southward until they had driven them to the south side of the Yellowstone, or Elk River, as it is known to the various Indian tribes of the plains.

Perhaps, in the first place, the Blackfeet coveted more than anything else the cliffs on the Two Medicine, — just above Holy Family Mission, — where the buffalo were decoyed in great numbers and stampeded in a huge waterfall of whirling brown bodies to death on the rocks below.

The Blackfeet call such a place — there were several of them — a *pi'skan,* a trap. Extending back from the cliff, for a mile or more out on the plain, were two ever-diverging lines of rock piles, like a huge letter V. Behind these the people concealed themselves, and the buffalo caller, going out beyond the mouth of the V, by certain antics and motions aroused the curiosity of the herd until it finally followed him into

The Thunder Medicine

the V. Then the people began to rise up behind it, and the result was that, unable to turn either to the right or left, from fear of the two lines of shouting, robe-waving stampeders, it was driven straight to the cliff and over it.

When I first saw the place, there were at the foot of the cliffs tons and tons of buffalo horn tips, the most time-resisting of any portion of a buffalo's anatomy.

Last night, while the pipe was going the rounds, I asked what had become of old Red Eagle's Thunder Medicine Pipe, and was told that it was still in the tribe, Old Person at present being the owner of it. Said Two Guns: "That is one of the most ancient and most powerful medicines we have. Do you know how it came into our possession?"

THE STORY OF THE THUNDER MEDICINE

"It was in the long ago. Our fathers had no horses then, but used dogs to carry their belongings.

"One spring, needing the skins of bighorn to tan into soft leather for clothing, the tribe moved up here to the foot of the Lower Two Medicine

Lake, and began hunting. Many men would surround and climb a mountain, driving the bighorn ahead of them, their dogs helping, and at last they would come up to the game, often several hundred head, on the summit of the mountain. The dogs were then held back, and the hunters, advancing with ready bow and arrows, would shoot and shoot the bighorn at close range and generally kill the most of them.

"One day, while most of the men were hunting, three young, unmarried women went out to gather wood, and while they were collecting it in little piles here and there, a thunderstorm came up. Then said one of them, a beautiful girl, tall, slender, long-haired, big-eyed, 'O Thunder! I am pure! I am a virgin! If you will not strike us I promise to marry you whenever you want me!'

"Thunder passed on, not harming them, and the young women gathered up their firewood and went home.

"On another day these three young women went out again for firewood, one ahead of another along the trail in the deep woods, and Mink Woman, she who had promised herself to Thunder Man, was last of the three. She was

The Thunder Medicine

some distance behind the others and singing happily as she stepped along, when out from the brush in front of her stepped a very fine-looking, beautifully dressed man, and said: 'Well, here I am. I have come for you.'

"'No, not for me! You are mistaken. I am not that kind; I am a pure woman,' she answered.

"'But you can't go back on your word. You promised yourself to me if I would not strike you, and I did not harm you. Don't you know me? I am Thunder Man.'

"Mink Woman looked closely at him, and her heart beat fast from fear. But he was good to look at, he had the appearance of a kind and gentle man, and — although thoughtlessly — she had made a promise to him, a god, and she could not break it. So she answered: 'I said that I would marry you. Well, here I am, take me!'

"Her two companions had passed on; they saw nothing of this meeting. Thunder Man stepped forward, and kissed her, then took her in his arms, and, springing from the ground, carried her up into the sky to the land of the Above People.

"But the two young women soon missed her. They ran back on the trail, and searched on all sides of it, and called and called to her, and of course got no reply: 'She may have gone home for something,' said one of them, and they hurried back to camp. She was not there. They then gave the alarm, and all the people scattered out to look for her. They hunted all that day, and wandered about in the woods all night, calling her name, and got no answer.

"The next morning Mink Woman's father, Lame Bull, made medicine and called in Crow Man, a god who sometimes lived with the people. 'My daughter, Mink Woman, has disappeared,' he told the god. 'Find her, even learn where she went, and you shall have her for your wife.'

"'I take your word,' Crow Man answered him. 'I believe that I can learn where she went. I may not be able to get her now, but I will some time, and then you will not forget this promise. I have always wanted her for my woman.'

"Crow Man went to the two young women and got them to show him where they had last seen Mink Woman. He then called a magpie to him, and said to the bird: 'Fly around here and find this missing woman's trail.'

"The bird flew around and around, Crow Man following it, and at last it fluttered to the ground, and looked up at him, and said: 'To this spot where I stand came the woman, and here her trail ends.'

"'Is it so!' Crow Man exclaimed. 'Well stand just where you are and move that long, shining black tail of yours. Move it up and down, and sideways. Twist it in every direction that you can.'

"The magpie did as he was told, and Crow Man got down on hands and knees, and went around, watching the shifting, wiggling, fanning tail. Suddenly he cried out: 'There! Hold your tail motionless in just that position!' and he moved up nearer and looked more closely at it. The sun was shining brightly upon it, and the glistening black feathers mirrored everything around. They were now spread directly behind the bird's body, and reflected the tree-tops, and the sky beyond them. Long, long, Crow Man stared at the tail, the people looking on and holding their breath, and at last he said to Lame Bull, 'I can see your daughter, but she is beyond my reach: I cannot fly there. She is up in sky land, and Thunder Man has her!'

"'*Ai! Ai!* She did promise herself to him the other day, if he would spare us,' one of the two wood gatherers said, 'but she did not mean it; she was only joking. It is no joke!'

"Lame Bull sat down and covered his head with his robe, and wept, and would not be comforted.

"Thunder Man took Mink Woman to sky land with him, and somehow, from the very first she was happy there with him; she seemed to forget at once all about this earth and her parents and the people. It was a beautiful land up there: warm and sunny, a country just like ours except that it had no storms. Buffalo and all the other animals covered the plains, and all sorts of grasses and trees and berry-bushes and plants grew there as they do here.

"But although Mink Woman was very happy there, Thunder Man was always uneasy about her, and kept saying to his people, 'Watch her constantly; see that she gets no hint of her country down below, nor sight of it. If she does, then she will cry and cry, and become sick, and that will be bad for me.'

"Thunder Man was often away, and during his absence his people kept a good watch on Mink Woman, and did all they could to amuse her; to keep her interested in different things.

The Thunder Medicine

One day a woman gave her some freshly dug *mas*,[1] and she cried out: 'Oh, how good of you to give me these! I must go dig some for myself!

" 'Oh, no! Don't go! We will dig for you all that you can use,' the women told her, but she would not listen.

" 'I want the fun of digging them for myself,' she told them. 'Somewhere, some time back, I did dig them. I must dig them again.'

" 'Well, if you must, you must,' they answered, and gave her a digging stick, and cautioned her not to dig a very large one, should she find it, for that *mas* was the mother of all the others, and was constantly bringing forth new ones by scattering her seed to the winds. She promised that she would not touch it, and went off happily with her digging stick and a sack.

"Well, Mink Woman wandered about on the warm grass and flower-covered plain, digging a *mas* here, one there, singing to herself, and thinking how much she loved her Thunder Man, and wishing that he would be more often at home. He was away the greater part of the time. Thus wandering, in a low place in the plain she came

[1] *Mas.* I know not the English name for this edible root. The French voyageurs' name for it was *pommes blanches.*

27

upon a *mas* of enormous size; actually, it was larger around than her body! 'Ha! This is the mother *mas*; the one they told me not to dig up,' she cried, and walked around and around it, admiring its hugeness.

"'I would like to dig it, but I must not,' she at last said to herself, and went on, seeking more *mas* of small size. But she could not forget the big one; she kept imagining how it would look out of the ground; on her back; in her lodge, all nicely cleaned and washed, a present for Thunder Man when he should return home. She went back to it, walked around it many times, went away from it, trying to do as she had been told. But when halfway home she could no longer resist the temptation: with a little cry she turned and never stopped running until she was beside it, and then she used the digging stick with all her strength, thrusting it into the ground around and around and around the huge growth and prying up, and at last it became loose, and seizing it by its big top leaves, she pulled hard and tore it from the ground, and rolled it to one side of the hole.

"What a big hole it was! And light seemed to come up through it. She stepped to the edge and looked down: upon pulling up the huge *mas* she had torn a hole clear through the sky earth! She stooped and looked through it, and there, far, far below, saw —

"Why, everything came back to her when she looked through it: There it was, her own earth land! There was the Two Medicine River, and there, just below the foot of its lower lake, was the camp of her people! She threw away her digging stick, and her sack of *mas*, and ran crying to camp and into Thunder Man's lodge. He was away at the time, but some of his relatives were in the lodge, and she cried out to them: 'I have seen my own country; the camp of my people. I want to go back to them!'

"Said Thunder Man's relatives to one another: 'She has found the big *mas*, and has pulled it up, and made a hole in our sky earth! Now, what shall we do? Thunder Man will be angry at us because we did not watch her more closely.' Thinking of what he might do to them in his anger, they trembled. They tried to soothe Mink Woman, but she would not be comforted; she kept crying and crying to be taken back to her father and mother.

"Thunder Man came home in the evening,

and upon learning what had happened, his distress was as great as that of Mink Woman, whom he loved. When he came into the lodge she threw herself upon him, and with tears streaming from her eyes, begged him to take her back to her people.

" 'But don't you love me?' he asked. 'Haven't you been happy here? Is n't this a beautiful — a rich country?'

" 'Of course I love you! I have been happy here! This is a good country! But oh, I want to see my father and mother!'

" 'Well, sleep now. In the morning you will likely feel that you are glad to be here, instead of down on the people's earth,' Thunder Man told her. But she would not sleep; she cried all night; would not eat in the morning, and kept on crying for her people.

"Then said Thunder Man: 'I cannot bear to see — to hear such distress. Because I love her, she shall have her way. Go, you hunters, kill buffalo, kill many of them, and bring in the hides. And you, all you women, take the hides and cut them into long, strong strips and tie them together.'

"This the hunters and the women did, and

The Thunder Medicine

Thunder Man himself made a long, high-sided basket of a buffalo bull's hide and willow sticks. This and the long, long one-strand rope of buffalo hide were taken to the hole that Mink Woman had torn in the sky earth, and then Thunder Man brought her to the place and laid her carefully in the basket, which he had lined with soft robes: 'Because I love you so dearly, I am going to let you down to your people,' he told her. 'But we do not part forever. Tell your father that I shall soon visit him, and give him presents I know that I did wrong, taking you from him without his consent. Say to him that I will make amends for that.'

" 'Oh, you are good, and I love you more than ever. But I must, I must see my people; I cannot rest until I do,' Mink Woman told him, and kissed him.

"The people then swung the woman in the basket down into the hole she had torn in the earth, and began to pay out the long rope, and slowly, little by little, the woman, looking up, saw that she was leaving the land of the sky gods. Below, the people, looking up, saw what they thought was a strange bird slowly floating down toward them from the sky. But after a long

31

time they knew that it was not a bird. Nothing like it had ever been seen. It was coming down straight toward the center of the big camp. Men, women, children, they all fled to the edge of the timber, the dogs close at their heels, and from the shelter of thick brush watched this strange, descending object. It was a long, long time coming down, twirling this way, that way, and swaying in the wind, but finally it touched the ground in the very center of the camp circle, and they saw a woman rise up and step out of it. They recognized her: Mink Woman! And as they rushed out from the timber to greet her, the basket which had held her began to ascend and soon disappeared in the far blue of the sky.

"All the rest of that day and far into the night, Mink Woman told her parents and her people about the sky gods and the sky earth, and even then did not tell it all. Days were required for the telling of all that she had seen and done.

"Not long after Mink Woman's return to the earth and her people, Thunder Man came to the camp. He came quietly. One evening the door curtain of Lame Bull's lodge was thrust aside,

The Thunder Medicine

and some one entered. Mink Woman, looking up from where she sat, saw that it was her sky god husband. He was plainly dressed, and bore a bundle in his arms: 'Father!' she cried; 'here he is, my Thunder Man!' And Lame Bull, moving to one side of the couch, made him welcome.

"Said Thunder Man: 'I wronged you by taking your daughter without your permission. I come now to make amends for that. I have here in this bundle a sacred pipe; my Thunder pipe. I give it to you, and will teach you how to use it, and how to say the prayers and sing the songs that go with it.'

"Said Lame Bull to this man, his sky god son-in-law, 'I was very angry at you, but as the snow melts when the black winds[1] blow, so has my anger gone from my heart. I take your present. I shall be glad to learn the sacred songs and prayers.'

"Thunder Man remained for some time, nearly a moon, there in Lame Bull's lodge, and taught the chief the ceremony of the medicine pipe until he knew it thoroughly in its every part. It is a powerful medicine,' Thunder Man told him. 'It will make the sick well; bring you and

[1] The "Chinook" wind. It is generally accompanied by dense black clouds that obscure the mountains.

your people long life and happiness and plenty, and success to your parties who go to war.'

"And as he said it was, so it proved to be, a most powerful medicine for the good of the people.

"Thunder Man's departure from the camp was sudden and unexpected. One evening he was sitting beside Mink Woman in Lame Bull's lodge, and all at once straightened up, looked skyward through the smoke hole, and appeared to be listening to something. The people there in the lodge held their breath and listened also, and could hear nothing but the chirping of the crickets in the grass outside. But Thunder Man soon cried out: 'They are calling me! I have to go! I shall return to you as soon as I can finish my work!' And with that he ran from the lodge and was gone. And Mink Woman wept.

"Who can know the ways of the gods? Surely not us of the earth. Thunder Man promised to return soon, but moons passed, two winters passed, and he came not to Lame Bull's lodge and his woman. But soon after he left so suddenly, Crow Man returned from far wanderings and heard all the story of the god and Mink

The Thunder Medicine

Woman. He made no remark about it, but spent much time in Lame Bull's lodge. Then, after many moons had passed, he said to the chief one day: 'Do you remember what you once promised me? When your daughter so suddenly disappeared you promised that if I would even find her, or tell you whither she had gone, you would give her to me when she was found. Well, here she is: fulfill your promise!'

" 'But she is no longer mine to give. She now belongs to Thunder Man,' the chief objected.

" 'Let me tell you this,' said Crow Man: 'You promised to give her to me if I would even tell you where she had gone. I did that. And now, as to this Thunder Man, he will never return here because he knows that I am in the camp, and he fears me. So you might as well give me your daughter now, as you will anyhow later.'

" 'Ask her if she will marry you. I agree to whatever she chooses to do,' Lame Bull answered.

"Crow Man went outside and found Mink Woman tanning a buffalo robe: 'I have your father's consent to ask you to marry me. I hope that you will say yes. I love you dearly. I will be good to you,' he told her.

"Mink Woman shook her head: 'I am already married. My man will soon be coming for me,' she answered.

" 'But if he doesn't come, will you marry me?' Crow Man asked.

" 'We will talk about that later. I will say now, though, that I like you very much. I have always liked you,' she replied.

"More moons passed, and as each one came, Crow Man never failed to ask Mink Woman to marry him. She kept refusing to do so. But after two winters had gone by, and Thunder Man still failed to appear and claim her, why, her refusals became faint, and fainter, until, finally, she would do no more than shake her head when asked the great question. Then, at last, in the Falling Leaves moon of the second summer, when Crow Man asked her again, and she only shook her head, he took her hand and raised her up and drew her to him and whispered: 'You know now that that sky god is never coming for you. And you know in your heart that you have learned to love me. Come, you are now my woman. Let us go to my lodge, my lodge which is now your lodge.'

"And without a word of objection Mink Woman went with him. Ai! She went gladly! She was lonely, and she had for some time loved him, although she would not acknowledge it.

"It was a good winter. Buffalo were plentiful near camp all through it, and Crow Man kept the lodge well supplied with fat cow meat. He and Mink Woman were very happy. Then came spring, and one day, in new green grass time, Thunder Man was heard approaching camp, and the people went wild with fear; they believed that he would destroy them all as soon as he learned that Mink Woman had married Crow Man. They all crowded around his lodge, begging him to give her up, to send her at once back to her father's lodge.

"But Crow Man only laughed: 'I will show you what I can do to that sky god,' he told them, and got out his medicines and called Cold-Maker to come to his aid. By this time Thunder Man was come almost to camp; was making a terrible noise just overhead. But Cold-Maker came quickly, came in a whirling storm of wind and snow. Thunder Man raged, shooting lightning, making thunder that shook the earth. Cold-Maker made the wind blow harder and harder, so that some of the lodges went down before it, and he caused the snow to swirl so thickly that the day became almost as dark as night. For a long time the two fought, light- ning against cold, thunder against snow, and little by little Cold-Maker drove Thunder Man back: he could not face the cold, and at last he fled and his mutterings died away in the distance. He was gone!

"'There! I told you I could drive him away,' said Crow Man. 'Mink Woman, you people all, rest easy: Thunder Man will never again at- tempt to enter this camp.' And with that he told Cold-Maker that he could return to his Far North home. He went, taking with him his wind and storm. The sun came out, the people set up their flattened lodges, and all were once more happy.

"And Lame Bull, he retained the pipe, and found that its medicine was as strong as ever. And from him it had been handed down from father to son and father to son to this day, and still it is strong medicine.

"Kyi! That was the way of it."

II

Pu-nak-ik-si (Cutbank)

July 18.

DOWN came our lodges this morning, and to-night we are camped in
Cutbank Canyon, just below the
great beaver ponds some six or seven miles from
the head of the stream. When I first saw these
ponds, years and years ago, they were dotted
with beaver houses, and at dusk one could
see the busy wood-cutters swimming from
them in all directions to their evening meal of
willow or quaking aspen bark, preparatory to
beginning their nightly work of storing food
for winter use. I never killed a beaver, but I
have torn down beaver dams in order to watch
the little animals repair them. Beavers have a
language as well as men: there was always a
chief engineer who told the workers just what
to do, and he himself rectified their mistakes.

We are encamped right on the main war road
of the Blackfeet into the country of the West
Side tribes. Once, when camped here with the

Blackfeet Tales of Glacier National Park

Small Robes (I-nuk´-siks), the band, or gens, of which I was a member, I saw a party of our young men make their preparations and start westward on a raid. They gathered in a sweat lodge with an old medicine man, who prayed earnestly for their success while he sprinkled the hot rocks with water, and dense steam filled the place. And at dusk, carrying in painted raw-hide cylinders their war finery, and in little sacks their extra moccasins, awl and sinew for repairs, and their little paint bags, they stole out in single file from the camp and headed for the summit of the range.

Every evening, during their absence, the old medicine man rode all through the camp, shaking his medicine rattles, singing the song for the absent, calling over and over each one's name, and praying for his safe return.

And then, one morning some two weeks later, they came into camp with a rush, driving before them sixty or seventy horses that they had taken from the Kootenais. And two carried a slender wand from which dangled a scalp. They came in singing the song of victory; and then the war chief shouted: "A multitude of the enemy are on our trail. Break camp, you

The Old War Road

women, and move down river. Take your weapons, you men, and turn back with us!"

We took our weapons. We mounted our horses and rode like mad up the old war trail, and within a half-hour sighted the enemy, forty or fifty of them, strung out in a long, straggling line, according to the strength and speed of each one's horse. We exchanged a few shots with the lead riders; one fell; the rest took their back trail, and how they did go up the steep incline to the summit, and over it. We did not pursue them: "Let them go!" Bear Chief shouted. "We have many of their horses; we have scalped three of them; let them go!"

We "let them go!" and, indeed, that was the wiser way: they could have made a stand at the summit and shot us down as fast as we came on.

The old war road! How many of my people have traveled over it, some of them never to return. It was along this road that Pitamakan, virgin woman warrior, led her warriors in what was to be her last raid! But how many, many times our people have come rushing homeward over it, singing their songs of victory, waving the scalps they have taken, and driving before them great bands of the horses of the

41

Blackfeet Tales of Glacier National Park

Pend d'Oreilles, the Snakes, the Nez Percés, and other tribes of the Columbia River watershed.

The names the Blackfeet have given to the four world directions are most significant of their entry into this Missouri River country. North is *ap-ut'-o-sohts:* back, or behind direction. South, *ahm-ska'-pohts,* is ahead direction. East is *pi-na'-pohts:* down river direction; and west is *ah-me'-tohts:* up-river direction. I have told why the Two Medicine was so named, when the Blackfeet came into the country from the Far North, and drove the Crows before them. This river they named Pu-nak'-ik-si (Cutbank), because its narrow valley for a long way up from its junction with the Two Medicine is walled in by straight-cut cliffs.

The Cutbank River Valley, like those of all the other streams of the country, has been the scene of many a fight between the Blackfeet and their enemies, in which the Blackfeet were generally the victors. A remarkable instance of an old woman's bravery occurred just below here some forty years ago.

A few lodges of the Kut'-ai-im-iks, or Never Laughs band of the Blackfeet, in need of the skins of elk and bighorn for making "buckskin"

An Old Woman's Bravery

for light clothing and moccasin tops, were here hunting, and one evening all the men gathered in old Running Crane's lodge for prayers with his beaver medicine. An old woman, named Muk-sin-ah´-ki (Angry Woman), was sitting in her lodge by herself because there had not been room for her in the crowded beaver medicine lodge. But she was listening to the distant singing, and saying over the prayers at the proper time, her heart full of peace and love for the gods.

As she sat there at the back of the lodge, she suddenly noticed that the doorway curtain in the upper part was being slowly pulled aside to the width of a hand, and in that small space an eye glared at her for a time, and then the curtain dropped back to place.

"That was the eye of an enemy," she said to herself. Her heart throbbed painfully; and for the time her thoughts were confused. Then, suddenly, some one, perhaps the sun himself, told her to take courage. She took courage: she stole out of the lodge to see what that enemy was doing. There was a moon; bright starlight; the night was almost as light as day; and she had no more than left the lodge than she saw the man walking here, there, examining the buffalo runners, the best and swiftest horses of the people, all picketed close to the lodges of their owners. Whenever the man's back was toward her, she hurried her steps; got closer and closer to him; and then, suddenly, she sprang and seized him from behind and shouted: "Help! Help! I have seized an enemy!"

In the beaver medicine lodge the men heard her and came running to her relief. She had the man down; he was struggling to rise; but the sun must have given her of his power: she held him firmly until they came, and they seized him, and White Antelope stabbed him to death. He was a Gros Ventre.

HOW MOUNTAIN CHIEF FOUND HIS HORSES

"Nephew, listen! Magic took place here in the long ago," said Yellow Wolf as we sat around his lodge fire this evening.

"The Ah´-pai-tup-i[1] were hunting on this Cutbank stream, every day or two moving nearer and nearer to the mountains. At one of their camping-places some distance below here, Mountain Chief lost his two fast buffalo runners, and although all the young men of the camp

[1] Ah'-pai-tup-i (Blood People). One of the twenty-four gentes of the Pi-kun'-i, or "Piegan" Blackfeet.

scattered out to look for them, they could not be found. Camp was moved nearer to the mountains, and after a few days moved again, this time to this very place where we are now encamped.

"The loss of the two buffalo runners was all that Mountain Chief could think about. As they could not be found, he felt sure that some enemy had stolen them.

"There was a Kootenai Indian visiting in camp, and one day he entered Mountain Chief's lodge, and said to him: 'You are grieving about the loss of your two fast horses. Now, if you will do as I say, perhaps I can find them for you.'

"'Whatever you ask, that shall be done,' Mountain Chief told him.

"'First, then, you must give me a robe, a good bow, and a quiver of arrows,' said the Kootenai.

"'They are yours; there they are: my own weapons, that robe. Take them when you want them,' said the chief.

"'I will take them later,' said the Kootenai. 'And now, call in your leading men.'

"Mountain Chief went outside and shouted the names of the men he wanted: a medicine man; several old, wise men; some warriors of great name. They came and were given seats in his lodge, each man according to his standing in the tribe. Said the Kootenai then: 'I have a sacred song that I want you all to learn. I will sing it over three or four times, then you sing it with me.'

"He sang the song. It was low in tone, and slow; a strange and beautiful song that gripped one's heart. But it was not hard to learn; after the Kootenai had sung it over four times, all there could sing it with him.

"Then the Kootenai told Mountain Chief to have the women build for him a little lodge there inside the big lodge. This they did by leaning sticks of two tripods against one of the poles of the lodge, their lower ends making a half-circle, and then covering them with buffalo leather. Into this little enclosure crept the Kootenai, taking with him a bird wing-bone whistle, and a medicine rattle, and as soon as was inside he ordered the women to smooth down carefully the leather coverings so that he would be in the dark. He then said to the people, sitting there in the big lodge: 'We will now sing the song four times. It is a call song to all living things: the birds, the animals, the trees, the rocks — yes, even they have life. All will come when we sing this song, and we will question them as to the whereabouts of the two missing horses.'

"They sang the song four times, and then the Kootenai, alone in his dark little lodge, sang another song, keeping time to it with his rattle, and the people, listening, heard outside the sighing of the wind through a big pine tree, although no such tree was near; and the Kootenai questioned the pine tree, and it answered that it had no knowledge of the missing horses.

"Then, at his summons, came the different birds and the animals; one could hear outside the flutter of their wings, the tread of their feet; and the Kootenai questioned them, and one by one they answered that they had not seen the horses. Came then a big rock, hurtling down through the sky and through the smoke hole of the lodge right into the fireplace, scattering ashes and coals all around the lodge, and frightening the people sitting there. And the Kootenai questioned it, and it answered that it knew nothing of the lost horses.

" 'Let us sing the sacred song again,' the Kootenai called out from his dark little lodge, and the people sang it with him, not once, but four times. The Kootenai then blew his whistle four times, four long, loud whistles. At the time there was no wind, but soon they heard, far off, the roar of an approaching wind of terrible force. Said the Kootenai then: 'I have called him, he is coming, Old-Man-of-the-Winds: be not afraid; he will not harm you.'

"He came with dreadful whirlwinds of his making. Winds that shook the lodge, and made the lodge ears hum with the noise of that of a hundred swarms of bees. And then, suddenly, the wind fell, and outside the people heard this wind god ask: 'Why have you sung — why have you whistled for me — what is it you want to know?'

"The Kootenai answered: 'Mountain Chief, here, has lost his two best horses. Fast buffalo runners they are; both black; one with a white spot on his side. I called you to ask if you have seen them anywhere?'

" 'No, I have not seen them,' Old-Man-of-the Winds answered. 'As you know, I belong on the west side of this Backbone-of-the-World. It is from there that I start the winds that blow over your country. I have been no farther

Mountain Chief and his Horses

out than here. No, I have not seen the horses.'

" 'Now I am depressed,' the Kootenai exclaimed. 'I did not expect to learn much about this from the birds, the animals, trees, and rocks, even the bumblebee could tell me nothing; but I felt that you would surely know where the two horses are!'

" 'Well, I have a friend who can tell you what you want to know,' said Old-Man-of-the-Winds. 'He is Red-Top Plume. He lives in the clouds; he can see the whole country; undoubtedly he can tell you where those horses are.'

" 'He is a stranger to me. How shall I find him — this Red-Top Plume?' the Kootenai asked; and all the people held their breath, waiting to hear the answer. Here was sacred talk; talk of a man with a god, and about gods; they could hardly believe that it was real, that which they were hearing.

"Answered Old-Man-of-the-Winds: 'Watch the clouds. When you see one of them turning from white to red, as the sun goes down to his lodge on his island in the great sea, you will know that Red-Top Plume is there above you. That red cloud is his plume. Yes, when you see that, sing your song again four times; blow your whistle again four times, and he will answer you.'

"And with that the wind suddenly started to blow from the east, and Old-Man-of-the-Winds went with it back to his western home, and they heard him no more.

"From his dark little lodge in the big lodge, the Kootenai called out to Mountain Chief: 'Go, stand outside your lodge, watch for a cloud turning red, and when you see it, come inside and tell me that it is there above us.'

"Mountain Chief went outside. He looked up and saw but a few small, white, slowly drifting clouds in the sky. There were four of them straight above him. These drifted toward one another, and he cried out: 'A sign! A sacred sign! Four small clouds are getting together to make one large cloud!'

"And at that all the people in the lodge cried out: 'The sacred number! Oh, sun! Oh, Above People all! Pity us! Pity us all! Allow us to survive all dangers! Give us long life and happiness!'

"And then, as the sun was setting, Mountain Chief cried out: 'The four are now one large cloud, and its edge is beginning to turn red! Ai! The red, the sacred color, spreads over it!'

"His voice trembled. Himself, he trembled;

Mountain Chief and his Horses

for he knew that he was looking — not at an ordinary cloud, but at Red-Top Plume himself, the great cloud god!

" 'Come in! Come in!' the Kootenai cried to him. And he went back into the lodge and joined in the singing of the sacred song. Four times they sang it, oh, how earnestly! The Kootenai then blew his wing-bone whistle four times. Followed a silence; the people scarcely daring to breathe. And then they heard outside, a deep and beautiful voice: 'I am Red-Top Plume! Why have you called me here?'

" 'Red-Top Plume! God of the clouds! Pity us!' the Kootenai answered. 'It is a matter of horses; of two fast buffalo runners; both black; one with a white spot on its side. We have lost them. Have you — oh, have you seen them anywhere?

" 'That is a small thing to call me down about,' the sky god answered; 'but, since I am here, I will tell you what I know: Yes, I have seen them. I saw them just now as I came down to earth. They are standing beside the spring just up the hill from where you camped when you lost them.'

" 'Ah! Ah! Ah!' the people exclaimed in

hushed voices. And the Kootenai, questioner of gods and unafraid, cried out: 'Red-Top Plume! Sacred plumed god of the clouds! You are good to us. Tell us, now, what we can do for you — what sacrifice to do?'

"But he got no answer. Red-Top Plume had gone — gone back to his home in the sky, and the people, rushing out from the lodge, looked up and saw him moving slowly eastward, his beautiful plumes redder than ever. And while the Kootenai and Mountain Chief and the other warriors made sacrifice to him, some young men mounted their horses and rode back to the camping-place where the two horses had been lost, and lo! they found them near the spring where Red-Top Plume had told that they were standing."

July 22.

Even in my day the many beaver dams in this wide canyon were in good repair, and the ponds were dotted with inhabited beaver lodges. There are few of the little woodcutters here now, but in time to come, under the sure protection of the supervisor of this Glacier National Park, they will become as numerous as they were before the white man came.

White Fur and his Beaver Clan

Talk about beavers to-night brought out a most interesting story by Tail-Feathers-Coming-over-the-Hill. Said he: "Beavers build a great dam, often working moons and moons to complete it. Then, when it is finished, and a great pond created, they build their lodges in the backed-up water, and cut their winter supply of cottonwood, willow, and quaking aspen, which they tow out in convenient lengths and sink in deep water around the lodges.

"Now, after a few winters, they have to move on and build another dam-and-pond, for they will have used up all the available trees and willows around the first pond. But that is still their pond, the clan that built it, and in time, when a new growth of food trees has sprung up around it, they return there, repair the dam, build new lodges, and remain as long as the young trees last."

WHITE FUR AND HIS BEAVER CLAN

"Away back in the ancient days, when our first fathers were able to talk with the animals, a beaver chief named White Fur, with his family and his relatives, built a big dam on this river. You can still see the remains of it, willow-grown, and it still backs up some water, a pond as large

53

in extent as the camp of our tribe. But in the old days that dam extended from one side to the other of the valley, and the water it backed up was more than a pond: it was a small lake. Above here, there is a swift stream of white water rushing down the north side of the valley from great ice banks in the mountains. Well, just below its junction with the river is where White Fur built the dam.

"Time passed. The sons of other beaver clans came and married the daughters of White Fur's clan, and took them off, and the sons of his clan went out and found wives and brought them home. The clan increased; the pond became full of lodges; the trees were cut in greater number each succeeding summer. So it was that, when the ice went out one spring, White Fur went around and around the pond, examining the remaining food trees, and saw that there remained only a few more than enough for the coming winter. It was no more than he expected; his last hurried look around, just before the freeze-up in the fall, had warned him that the food supply was getting small.

THE BEAVER DAM

Blackfeet Tales of Glacier National Park

"He went home, and called a council, told what he had learned on his round, and then said: —

"'We must move out from here as soon as the ice breaks up next spring, and when we go we must know just where we are going; we cannot afford to lose time hunting for a good place to make a new home. Now, who will start out on discovery?'

"'I will!' his eldest son, Loud Slap, first answered. He was so named because he could tail-slap the water louder than any one else in whole gens.

"Now, Loud Slap was White Fur's favorite son and next to himself the best, the wisest dam-builder in the gens. The chief wanted to keep him at home, for going on discovery was very dangerous. But for very shame he could not order him to remain and let some other take the risk. So, with sinking heart, he said: 'You spoke up first, my son, so you shall be the first one to look for a new home for us. I have had a dream, and I want you to find out if it told me truth: Go down this river a little way beyond the edge of the pines, look north, and you will see a big ridge with a low gap in it. Go up through that gap, and down the other side, and you will soon come to a small branch of a good-sized stream; look at all the branches of that stream for a good home for us, and come back and tell us all about it. Make that crossing through the gap in the daytime, for then the most of our enemies, the mountain lion, the fisher and the wolverine, the wolf and the coyote, are generally asleep. Night is the time that they do their murdering work.'

" 'As you say, so I will do,' Loud Slap answered.

"And the next morning, some time before daylight, he started down river on his dangerous trail of discovery. Below his pond there were other ponds; and as he swam through them many of the beavers living in them asked him where he was going.

" 'Out on discovery; our food trees will last us only this coming winter; we have to find a new home,' he answered them all.

"On he went, through the last of the ponds, down the river, swimming fast, so very fast that his big webbed hind feet, swiftly kicking, made the water foam past his breast. He had started out too early; when he passed the last of the pines, daylight was still some time off, so he dived under a pile of driftwood, then crawled up into it, found a good resting-place on one of the logs and went to sleep, sure that none of the prowlers could reach him there.

"The sun shining down through the little openings in the driftwood pile awakened him. He slipped down into the water, made a dive, and came up out in the middle of the river. Near by was a high, sloping bank bare of trees and brush; he swam to shore, climbed it, looked north, and saw the big ridge and the big, low gap in it. He looked all around; no animals were in sight except a few elk, and he knew that they would not harm him: he began waddling toward the gap.

"The sun was hot. Loud Slap's legs were short; his body fat and heavy; there was no water; he soon became very tired and thirsty, and the top of the gap seemed to be a long way off. More and more often he had to stop and rest, but he kept saying to himself: 'I will not give up! I will not give up!' — and at last he arrived at the top of the gap. Close up to the top on the other side were thick, cool groves of quaking aspen and willows; as far as he could

White Fur and his Beaver Clan

see, the valley below him and its far side was one green growth of trees, and he knew that somewhere down there was water, plenty of it. Down he went, oh, how easily, on the steeper places just pushing a little with his hind feet and sliding along on his belly. He soon came to a small stream of running water and drank and drank of it, rolled over and over in its shallowness until wet all over, and then he followed it down. Other little streams came into it, and at last it became so deep that he could swim. After a time he came to where this stream joined a much larger one, and he turned and went up it, and away up in the timber found where a dam could be built that would form a very large pond, and best of all the quaking aspens and willows were everywhere there growning so closely together that they formed a food supply that would last a number of winters.

"That night Loud Slap slept in a hold that he dug in a bank of the stream. This is the one which we long ago named Ki-nuk´-si Is-si-sak´-ta. I understand that the white people have another name for it.[1]

"Early next morning Loud Slap came out of his hole, cut down a small quaking aspen, and

[1]Ki-nuk´-si Is-si-sak´-ta (Little River). By the whites named Milk River.

59

ate all he wanted of its bark. He then swam down the stream, turned up its little fork, and before the sun was very high left it and took his back trail up through the gap, and before noon was going down the long slope to Cutbank River. The going was easy. But one thing troubled him: the risk that he ran traveling there in that open, waterless country. Whenever he came to a patch of buck brush or a clump of tall grass, he would sit up and look all around to see if any enemy was near; and then he would go on, keeping as close to the ground as possible. Twice he saw a coyote in the distance, and sat motionless until the animal moved on out of sight. And then, when almost to the river, sitting up and looking out from a brush patch, he saw a wolverine coming straight toward him. He trembled; he shivered. 'Now is my end come!' he said to himself, and imagined how it was going to feel to be bitten and clawed and torn to death. Because of his helplessness, because he could in no way defend himself, he wept; but silently.

"On came the wolverine, sniffing the ground; sniffing the rocks; the weed growths; and once, when he turned and looked back, Loud Slap

White Fur and his Beaver Clan

threw himself flat there in the brush; he had not dared move before. The wind was from the southwest; the wolverine was coming from the west, and that was one thing in Loud Slap's favor. But on which side of that patch of brush would he pass? If to the north, then he would scent the beaver-odor trail, follow it, and all would be over. If he passed to the south of the patch, and not too close, then all would be well. From where he lay, flat on the ground in the brush, Loud Slap could see nothing but the brush stems in front of his nose; but presently he heard, close to the patch and to the west of it, the sniff! sniff! sniffle! of his enemy. He closed his eyes; his body shook with fear; he could almost feel strong, sharp-fanged jaws closing upon neck! The suspense was terribly hard to bear! And then, after what seemed to be a whole moon of time, he heard the sniffling close in front of him; then faint and fainter off in the direction of the river; and presently he opened his eyes, little by little rose up, and looked out from his hiding-place. Lo! Wolverine had come close, *close* to the brush patch, and south of it, and then had turned, and was now walking slowly toward the river! 'My enemy passes! I survive!'

Blackfeet Tales of Glacier National Park

Loud Slap said to himself, and would have sung had he dared. Oh, yes, beavers sang in those days, as you shall learn.

"Loud Slap watched the wolverine go on down the valley, and then waddled to the river as fast as he could work his legs. How good it felt, that plunge into the cool water from the bank! And, once into it, he made it foam as he swam homeward against the swift current. Long before night he climbed the dam of the upper pond, and a little later entered his father's lodge. 'Ha! Back so soon! What found you, my son?' old White Fur asked.

"'A fine stream there on the other side of the gap. A place to dam a large pond. Plenty of food bark trees,' Loud Slap answered, and then told carefully all about the place, and about his narrow escape from the wolverine. Then his mother went swimming from lodge to lodge of the gens, calling all the heads of the families, and when they had gathered in White Fur's lodge he told again of his find and of the dangers of the trail. All went home pleased that he had found such a good place for a new home for them.

White Fur and his Beaver Clan

"White Fur and his whole gens worked very hard that summer to get in sufficient food bark sticks for the winter supply. They had to drag the last of them a long way to water, and they kept at it long after the snow came, and until the ice and cold weather prevented further cutting. The trails they left in the snow, just before the pond froze over, were a sure call to their passing enemies, and they halted and lay in wait beside them, and killed in all five of the members of the gens, one of them Loud Slap's oldest son. A lynx was seen to spring upon him and carry him off, as he was going out to finish cutting down a large tree.

"The winter passed. When spring came, there was still considerable food bark untouched on the underwater piles, but, oh, how glad the beavers were to be able to swim about again, and eat fresh bark from living tree branches. All were anxious to start at once for the new home across the ridge, but white Fur would not permit it. From the pressure of the winter snows the dead grass of the past summer lay flat: 'We must wait until the new grass grows high enough to conceal us,' he said, 'and then we will go.'

Blackfeet Tales of Glacier National Park

"Of course, he meant those that would be able to go: females with newborn young were to remain where they were until the young should be old enough to travel, and then they were to cross the ridge and join their mates. The new grass came, and when it was a little higher than the top of a beaver's back, old White Fur and Loud Slap led all those who could go, about fifty of them, down the river on the way to the stream beyond the gap. White Fur had already talked with the chief who lived in the next pond below, and he had promised to keep all newcomers from occupying the pond that White Fur and his gens were leaving for a time.

"The travelers saw no enemy on the trail up through the gap, and, upon arriving at the place that Loud Slap had discovered, were well pleased with it. That very evening, after a heavy meal of bark, they began work on the dam, and morning had much willow brush laid, butts to the current, across the stream. Night and day, with little rest, they toiled to complete the dam, of sticks and stones and sod and earth, and within two moons' time they finished it, and had a pond large enough and

White Fur and his Beaver Clan

deep enough for the lodges of the gens, and all the food sticks they would need to sink for winter use. Then, one evening, came those who had been left behind, came with their strong and half-grown young, and all began at once to cut and bring in and sink the winter food supply. Long before winter set in they had stored more than they could possibly use, and from that time until the ice formed they did nothing more than strengthen the dam, and eat and sleep, and play about in the water.

"The winter passed, and more young were born. Came and went another winter, and in the spring more young were born. There were now in the gens many two, and three, and some four year-olds, both male and female, and they could not mate with one another; something had to be done for them. Old White Fur called a council, and there was much talk about it. Some favored sending scouts away down the Little River to learn if there were any beaver colonies along it. Others, and the greater number, declared that the unmarried males should take the trail through the gap down to Cutbank River, find mates in the different gens having ponds along it, and tell the unmarried males there to come over and take wives from White Fur's gens. It was decided that this should be done, and one morning more than forty young males started for Cutbank River.

"Days passed; and yet more days, and no wife-seeking beavers came to the pond on Little River. 'Something is wrong,' White Fur told Loud Slap.

"'*Ai!* Something is wrong. If none come within four days' time, I shall go over to the Cutbank ponds and learn what the trouble is.'

"The four days passed, and no stranger, not one, came. On the fifth morning Loud Slap once more took the trail for Cutbank, saying to White Fur as he left, 'If I do not return within four days' time, then send some one over to learn what the trouble is, for I shall be dead.'

"Down the river went Loud Slap, and up the little fork, and thence along the trail through the gap in the ridge. He moved along very cautiously, keeping a sharp lookout in all directions, and seeing nothing to alarm him. After passing through the gap he saw, on a ridge to the east, a number of wolves following a small bank of buffalo, and that pleased him, for, seeking food there, they would not be likely to turn and cross his trail. He hurried on down the slope.

"Suddenly, when near the river, a whirl of wind brought a dreadful odor to his nostrils; an odor of dead and decaying flesh. He stopped, sat up, looked sharply ahead, saw nothing to alarm him, went on a short distance, and came upon a scene that made him shiver; that made him mourn: there on the trail and on both sides of it, lay his youthful kin who had gone out to seek wives! There they lay, their bodies swollen and bursting, every one of them mangled and torn, several half eaten by their enemies, wolves probably, that had discovered and killed them all! One look at them was enough; he hurried on, weeping, and plunged into the river.

"Upstream he went, faster than he had ever swam before, and soon entered the lower one of the beaver ponds. Straight to the chief's lodge he swam, and dived down to the entrance, and went up into the big and comfortable grass-floored home.

"'Ha! Loud Slap! It is you! Welcome you are! Sit youth and give us the news!' the chief cried out.

"Loud Slap greeted him and gave the news, and both wept over the death of so many of their kind. The chief's wife went out and spread the news, and there was mourning in every lodge in that pond.

"The chief then gave Loud Slap bad news. Said he: 'In the early part of this moon came to us a visitor form the big pond at the head of the lake on the next stream south of this river.' He meant, of course, the great beaver pond just above Lower Two Medicine Lake.

"'Yes?' said Loud Slap, — 'yes?'

"'Ah! He came and visited us and our kin in the other ponds, and gave no reason for his coming, and soon went home. But in a few days' time he returned with all his gens, and they are many, and took possession of the upper pond, your pond, and at this time they are re- pairing the dam and backing the water up into the new growth of food trees, which are as thick as they can stand. We told him, we all told him, this chief — Strong Dam is his name, — that he should not take the pond, as it belongs to you, to your father, White Fur, and his gens. But he said that he did not care who owned it, he had taken it, and would hold it, fight for it against all comers.'

"'Ha! Is it so!' Loud Slap cried. 'We will see about that! Say nothing to any one that I have been here. Tell your people to keep my visit secret from all above here. I go to bring my kindred over, and we will drive that Strong Dam and his gens back whence they came, or kill them all.'

"Loud Slap went back to his Little River home the next day, and told all that he had seen and learned. All mourned and mourned for their dead, and their hearts burned with anger against Strong Dam and his gens. Said White Fur: 'I am old, old. But I can still fight! We will go over to our pond to-morrow. I will lead you, and we will teach that Strong Dam and his relatives something; we will send them crying back to their pond above the lake!'

"They started the next morning, all the males, and even females that were without young; and they were many, those who were waiting for males of other gentes to come and marry them. Old White Fur led them across to the river without mishap, and up to the first pond, where they visited, and rested, and ate their fill of fresh, green bark. And there some of the females met young unmarried males who wanted to mate with them; and they answered, 'We will marry you, but first you must fight for us; you must help us drive that Strong Dam and his gens from our pond.'

"'And is that all you ask?' they replied. 'We are only too glad to help you. Who would not fight for his sweetheart should not have one!'

"This gave White Fur something to think about; and after a time he said to Loud Slap: 'Go, now, on a secret mission: visit the ponds of our friends above here, and say to the unmarried males that our young females here will marry them, but they must first help us drive Strong Dam from this river.'

"'Ai! That is a good plan,' said Loud Slap; and he started at once to carry it out. Late that night he returned, and reported that all the young males had agreed to the proposal, and would join White Fur and his kin when they came along.

"'Let us start now,' said White Fur; and the advance began, and by the time he reached the dam of his own old pond, he had a large following.

"There was a young man lying there on

White Fur and his Beaver Clan

the dam, a far-back ancestor of ours who had gone there to get his medicine dream; his vision. He was awake; and when, in the bright moonlight, he saw that big, old, white-furred beaver come up on the dam, and a hundred and more beaver following, he could not believe his eyes, and cried out: 'Am I really and truly awake, or is this a medicine vision?'

"'Hush! Keep still,' old White Fur told him. 'What you see is real. We are come to fight and drive off those here who have stolen our pond and our new growth of food trees. Just you keep still: we want to surprise them. If you see that they are beating us, then give us help. When all is over, I will give you a medicine that will insure you long life and happiness.'

"The young man — No Otter was his name — made signs that he would keep quiet. And he sat there and watched more than a hundred beavers cross the dam close in front of him, and slide quietly into the pond, and even then could hardly believe that he was not dreaming.

"As they entered the water that great war party of beavers swam out in all directions for the shores of the pond, where, scattered all along, Strong Dam and his kin were already cutting the young trees for winter food. And as he watched and listened, the young man heard suddenly a great commotion and squealing all along the shore: the fighting had begun. Then, almost at once, the attacked and the attackers took to the water, and the whole surface of the pond was as if it had been struck by a tornado. It boiled, and eddied, and foamed, and shot high in spray, and with it all was the slap! slap! slap! of beaver tails as the animals struggled and clinched, and floundered and bit, all over its long length and width. And soon beavers, frightened and gasping for breath, and bleeding from many wounds, began to pass on each side of the young man over the dam, and drop into the stream below and disappear in its swift current. And some, unable to climb it, and bleeding from many wounds, died there at the edge of the dam and sank. The water was red with their blood. One of them, crawling out, staggered right up against the young man, and gasped, and died, and he put out his hand and felt of it, its wet coat, the warm but now breathless body, and then for the first time was he sure that what he was witnessing was real, and no dream.

White Fur and his Beaver Clan

"The fight was over. The last of the enemy had been killed, or had fled down river, and White Fur and his party gathered on the dam. Not all were there: some of them lay dead on the bottom of the pond or sorely wounded on the shore. White Fur directed that they should be helped into the cool lodges, where they would be safe from the prowlers, and there cared for and fed. That done, said White Fur to the young man: 'You have seen a great sight this night. Had we needed your help I know that you would have given it.'

"'Yes, you had but to call, and I would have been with you,' the young man answered.

"'I know it,' said White Fur, 'and just for your good-will I shall give you a strong medicine and teach you the songs that go with it. But I cannot do this here; you will have to go home with us, to our pond on the next stream to the north.'

"They went there the next day, leaving behind the newly married females and their mates to care for the wounded and make them well. And on the way up through the gap and down to the pond, White Fur and Loud Slap told the young man the story of their lives and their troubles, just as I am telling it to you. And upon reaching the pond on Little River, No Otter remained there a long time with the beavers, the old chief and his son, Loud Slap, giving him a medicine beaver cutting and teaching him the beaver songs. It was a good medicine. He took it home with him, and kept it, and made ceremony with it, and sang the songs as he had been taught to do, and because of that he had great success at war, and in curing the sick, and he lived to great age.

"Kyi! So ends my story."

July 25.

Yesterday Guardipe, or, as I prefer to call him, Ai´-is-an-ah-mak-an (Takes-Gun-Ahead), climbed with me to the top of White Calf Mountain. There, on the extreme summit of the rough crested mountain, we came upon five bighorn, all ewes, and not one of them with a lamb beside her. During the lambing season here this year there was a continuous downpour of rain and sleet and snow, in which the newborn young undoubtedly perished.

But how tame those five ewes were! We walked to within fifty yards of them, and they

An Escape from a Grizzly

gazed at us curiously, now and then nervously
stamping the rock with one or the other of their
fore feet. And then they circled around us, twice,
and finally walked off toward the eastern point
of the mountain, often stopping to look back at
us, and finally disappeared behind some rock piles.

At the same time Kut´-ai-ko-pak-i (No-Cow-
ard-Woman — as my people have named my
wife) was having her own experience with the
game in this Park. With Miss L——, a Boston
friend, she was sitting near the edge of a high,
almost cutbank at the edge of the river, when she
heard the slow, heavy, twig snapping tread of an
animal back in the brush. She gave her friend a
nudge, and pointed in the direction of the sounds,
and the two watched and listened. And presently
they saw the brush shaking as the animal forced
its way through it, and then, half revealed and
half concealed in more open brush, they saw a
big grizzly coming straight toward them! Right
near where they sat a dwarf juniper grew at the
edge of the high bank, several of its limbs overhanging it. Without speaking a word, and
trembling as though they had ague, they crept
to the tree, grasped one of the limbs, and tena-
ciously gripping it let themselves down over the

edge of the bank. And then — the limb broke with a loud snap and down they went along the gravelly incline, so steep that they could get no foothold, over and over, head first, feet first, and sideways, and landed in the river with a loud splash. But they did not mind that: what were bruises and a wetting compared to being mauled by a grizzly? They forded the waist-deep stream and arrived dripping but safe in camp, and were glad to be there!

Although this Glacier National Park is only five years old, the game animals within it have already become very tame. The bighorn and the Rocky Mountain goats no longer flee from parties traversing the moutain trails, and the deer and elk and moose have become almost as fearless as they are. As for the bears, they are continually trying to break into the meat-houses of the different camps. Undoubtedly these mountains and forests within the next ten years will fairly be alive with game. And as to trout, the supply is increasing instead of decreasing. In this Cutbank stream alone there have been caught this season in the neighborhood of two thousand trout, weighing from a fourth of a pound up to four pounds, but since the 1st of April seventy

The Story of the Bad Wife

thousand young trout, from the Anaconda hatchery, have been put into it.

Last night, in Black Bull's lodge, we had more tales of the long ago in this Cutbank Valley. Would that I had the time to collect all the Blackfeet legends of the various places in their once enormous domain. From the Saskatchewan to the Yellowstone, and from the Rockies between these two streams, eastward for about three hundred miles, there are tales of adventure, of camp-life, and wonderful legends, for every mountain, stream, butte, and spring within that great area. Said Black Bull last night: —

"I will tell you a story that my grandfather told me. It happened in the days of his fathers' boyhood, and it is called

"THE STORY OF THE BAD WIFE

"One summer in that time the people, having made new lodges, moved up here on Cutbank River to cut new lodge poles, and to gather weasel-eyes[1] which grew in great quantities back on the high mountain slopes.

"At that time one of the best-liked young men of the tribe was Falling Bear. He was a very

[1] Ap-ah a-wap-spi. Weasel-eyes: huckleberries.

77

brave and successful warrior, and very kind-hearted: he took it upon himself to keep three or four old widows and several old and helpless men supplied with all the meat and skins they could use, and even gave them gentle horses for packing and riding whenever camp was moved. At the time the people moved up here on Cutbank, he had been married but a short time. He had fallen in love with Otter Woman, the most beautiful girl in the tribe, and with her father's and mother's consent, and to their great joy and pride, had set up with her a lodge of his own. No word had been so much as whispered against Otter Woman; she was believed to be as good and pure as she was beautiful of face and form.

"The tribe had not been here many days when Falling Bear decided to go to war. Many of the warriors, some of them much older than he, wanted to go with him, but he told them all that this time, because of a dream, a vision he had, he would take no one but his woman. He made full preparation for the war trail, had a sacred sweat with an old medicine man, who was to pray for him during his absence, and then, with his woman, he took the Cutbank trail for the

The Story of the Bad Wife

country of the West Side tribes, all of them enemies of the Blackfeet.

"Traveling with great caution, and only at night, he passed through the country of the Flatheads, and came to the plains country of the Nez Percés. There he struck the trail of a big hunting party of people, and followed it, and soon found that he was gaining upon them; one early morning he came upon their camping-place which they must have left on the previous afternoon, for in some of the fireplaces there were still live coals deep down in the ashes.

"Now, on the night before he had lost his tobacco, and his desire to smoke was strong within him. So he said to his woman, 'You go around on that side of the big camping-place and examine every lodge site for tobacco leavings, and I will search this side for it.' They parted and began their quest.

"The camp had been pitched partly in an open, grassy park, and partly in the timber surrounding it; and because of that Falling Bear and his woman were often out of sight of each other. At one of these times Otter Woman was examining a lodge site and fireplace back in the timber, and, happening to look off to one side, she saw hanging on some brush a fine shield, some beautiful war clothes, and a large fringed and painted medicine pouch. She well knew that these had been spread out to sun by the campers and forgotten, and that some one would be coming back for them, and was about to go after Falling Bear to come and take them when she heard the tread of an approaching horse. So near was it that she had not time to run and hide. She stood still, staring, and almost at once there came in sight, on a black-and-white pinto horse, the handsomest young man that she had ever seen. He was so handsome that to look at him gave her a yearning pain in the heart for him. Just one look, and she had fallen in love with him! She did n't want to fall in love with him; she just could n't help it!

"He, this Nez Percé, checked up his horse and sat quiet, staring down at her, and no doubt thought her the handsomest woman he had ever seen. Suddenly she began making signs to him. What a wonderful thing that silent language is! All the tribes of the plains know it. Just by the use of their hands they can express their every thought to one another.

The Story of the Bad Wife

"Signed she: "My man is over there! Be quiet. I will go to him, somehow get his weapons from him, then hold him. You come quickly when I cry out, and kill him, and I will go with you; will be your woman.'

"Of course, nothing could have pleased the Nez Percé more than that. To kill an enemy and take his beautiful woman, what a big *coup* that would be! He signed to the woman that what she proposed was good, and slid from his horse and tied it to a tree, then signed to her to go, and he would follow, keeping out of sight.

"The woman crossed the big camping-ground and found her man: 'I have made a great find,' she told him. 'On some bushes over there are hanging beautiful war clothes, a shield, weapons, and a medicine pouch. Leave you your weapons and things here, and come with me, and take them.'

"'But why should I leave my weapons? One should never be without them,' he objected.

"'Because from here goes the trail we are to follow, and you will have all you can do to bring here what I have found,' she explained.

"He did n't see any sense in leaving his weapons, but took her word and laid them down, along with his medicine pouch, and his war clothes in their *parflèche* (painted cylinder), and followed her out into the open park. 'The things are right across there in the brush,' she told him, pointing to the place, and then gradually dropped back to his side, and then a step behind him. Then, as they came near the brush on the far side, she suddenly seized him, endeavoring to squeeze his arms close to his side, so that he could not use them, and at the same time she called out to the Nez Percé to come to her assistance. He had been watching, and was already coming as fast as he could run.

"Falling Bear, of course, saw at once the intentions of the two, and as quick as a flash of lightning made up his mind what to do. He only half struggled with the woman, now grasping his neck with one hand and arm, and beating his eyes and face with the other hand. She was fast blinding him, but he stood the pain of it until the Nez Percé, with war club raised, was but a step or two away. He then broke loose from the woman, kicked backward, his foot striking her in the stomach and knocking her over, and then he sprang at the Nez Percé, seized the arm and hand

The Story of the Bad Wife

that held the war club high, and struggled with the man for possession of it. He wrenched it away from him and with it struck him a hard blow on the head, and he fell, his skull crushed in, and died. The victor scalped him with his own knife, took his war club and his bow and arrows, and then turned to the woman.

"She lay where she had fallen, trembling at what she had done, wishing that she had not done it. 'Get up. If you spoke truth, if there are war clothes and other things over there, lead me to them,' Falling Bear told her.

"She arose, still trembling, but now with some hope that he was not going to kill her, and led him to the place. His eyes were swelling shut so fast that one was entirely closed, but he could partly use the other. He looked at the things there on the brush: 'Ah! Here are the war clothes, the shield, the medicine pouch, but where are the weapons?' he asked.

"The woman did not answer. What could she say? There had been no weapons left on the brush. Falling Bear laughed a laugh that made her shiver, and told her to gather up all that was there and follow him. He unfastened the horse and led it across the camping-place, she following, and he had her take up his own weapons and things and fasten them to the saddle. He then mounted the horse, and told her to lead it and take the back trail home. Before he had ridden far his other eye closed; he was, for the time, wholly blind; but not afraid. He kept close possession of all the weapons, and made the woman do everything that he wanted done. She minded his every word.

"Traveling again at night, and hiding in the brush during the daytime, the two passed safely through the country of the Flatheads, and crossed the mountains. On the morning that they approached the camp here on Cutbank, Falling Bear had partly recovered the use of one eye. The other was still swollen shut; it seemed to have been poisoned by the woman's fingernails.

"When so near the camp that they could plainly see the lodges, Falling Bear told the woman to go on in and tell her relatives to come to him; that he would await them, right where he was. They soon came out to him, his father-in-law and his brother-in-law, and when they saw his scarred face and swollen eyes, they cried out:

The Story of the Bad Wife

'Oh, what has happened to you? Have you been in a fight with a mountain lion?'

" 'Worse than that,' he answered; 'this was done to me by the one I most loved and trusted! And then he told them all about it, and concluded by giving them the horse and all the things that he had taken from the Nez Percé.

"When he finished his awful tale the two men, listening closely, were so overcome with shame and grief that for a time they could not speak. But at last Falling Bear's father-in-law said: 'I have made up my mind what to do. Come! Let us go on into camp.'

"They went in; Falling Bear to his own lodge — in which his father and mother lived. His woman was not there; she had gone to her father's lodge. He was glad that she had gone there; he never wanted to see her again. His father asked him to give the story of his war trail, and he answered that he had nothing to say. He was so sick at heart that he could not talk.

"Arrived in his own lodge, and finding his daughter, Otter Woman, there, Falling Bear's father-in-law told her to go out for a time; and when she was gone he told her mother all that she had done, and then, calling in their son, the three agreed upon the way the bad wife should be punished. They called her in and told her to braid her hair nicely, and to put on her best clothes. And while she was doing that, her father and mother and brother painted their faces black and let down their hair.

"As soon as Otter Woman was dressed, her father said to her: 'We will now go outside, and you will mount the Nez Percé horse. I will lead it, your mother and brother will follow, and we will go all through the camp, stopping here and there to tell the people all about the great wrong you did your man.'

"'Oh, no, no! Not that!' Otter Woman cried. 'I am ashamed enough as it is! I am sorry that I did it! I don't know how I came to do it; I shall never, never do such a thing again!'

"'You spoke the truth there,' said her father. 'No, you will never do it again!' And he ordered her to go out ahead of them and mount the horse. She did so and sat upon it, head cast down, looking neither to the right nor left nor ahead: shame was with her. Holding the horse's rope, the old man shouted: 'Listen, people, listen.' And when a crowd had gathered he told

The Story of the Bad Wife

them what his daughter had done to her good man, and the people groaned with shame that one of their tribe could be so bad of heart. Some even wept at the horror of it.

"From one part of the camp to another the old man led the little procession, stopping often to tell the shameful story, until all knew it. And then at last he led the horse out into the center of the great circle of the lodges, and told his daughter to dismount. She did so, and, drawing his knife, he stabbed her in the heart and she fell and died. Said he then to his wife: 'Get women to help you; drag that body far off and leave it, and never let me hear again the name of her who was once my daughter!'

"And the women did as he said. Never again did any one mention Otter Woman in his presence."

"Ai! A sad story! A story to give one bad dreams! Let us have one of more cheerful nature before we go to bed," said Stabs-by-Mistake.

"An Old Man story, then," said Two Guns. "All are laughable."

"Elder brother, tell us the story of Old Man and the woman," said Black Bull to Tail-Feathers-Coming-over-the-Hill.

87

BLACK BULL AND STABS-BY-MISTAKE (RIGHT)
NEAR LOWER END OF CUTBANK CAÑON

Old Man and the Woman

"Ai! That I will," the chief answered.

But before I set down the story, I must explain Old Man.

Old Man (Näp´-i) was the god who created the world, and all life upon it, and he was *the* god of the Blackfeet until, some centuries back, they got from some southern tribe another religion, of which the sun is the principal god. However, they still pray to Old Man, as well as to the gods of the later religion, although in time a great many stories have grown up about Old Man that make him appear to be more of a buffoon than a god. An interesting point about the word *näp´-i* is, that, while it is the term for an old man, its real meaning is dawn, or the first faint, white light that gives birth to the day. And so, in common with the ancient Mexicans, various tribes of the plains, the Aryans and other ancient races of the Old World, the original religion of the Blackfeet was the worship of light personified.

Let us have now, the old chief's story of

OLD MAN AND THE WOMAN

"Having created the world, the animals, grass, trees, all life upon it, Old Man realized that by having men live by themselves, and women by themselves, he had made a mistake. He saw that they should live together. The camps of the two sexes were far apart: the women were living here at the foot of the mountains, in Cutbank Valley, and the men were away down on Two Medicine River. Each camp had a buffalo trap, and subsisted wholly upon the buffalo that were decoyed into it.

"As I have said, Old Man saw that he had made a mistake in keeping men and women apart. In fact, he found that he himself wanted a woman; so he went to the men and said: 'You shall no longer live by yourselves. Come! We will go up to the camp of the women, and each of us get one of them.'

"The men were more than glad to do that; it was what they had been hoping to do for a long time; so they hurried to put on their best clothes, and neatly braided their hair, and then started off with Old Man for the women's camp. When they came in sight of it, Old Man told them to stop right there, and he would go ahead and plan with the women just what should be done. They sat down, and he went on to the women's camp. Himself, he had on his old, soiled clothes;

Old Man and the Woman

his fine clothes he had left back with the men.

"Arrived in the camp, he found only two or three women there; the woman chief and all the others were down at the buffalo trap, butchering the animals that they had that morning decoyed into it. When he told the few women that he found why he had come, he greatly excited and pleased them, and they started at once to run and tell the others to hurry up from the trap and meet the men.

" 'But wait. Not so fast. I want a word with you,' Old Man called out; and when they came back to him, he asked: 'What kind of a woman is your chief?'

" 'Everything that is good, and kind and brave, that is our chief,' one answered. And another said: 'Ai! She is all that, and more; and she is the most beautiful woman of us all!'

"This pleased Old Man. He said to himself, 'That is the woman for me. I must have her.' And to the waiting women he said: 'It is right that chief woman should mate with chief man. You women are to come to us, and each select the man you want. Now, tell your chief woman that the chief man is brave and kind and handsome, and that she shall select him for her man.

91

She will know him by the way he is dressed. He wears buckskin shirt and leggings, embroidered with porcupine quills, and a cow-leather robe with a big porcupine-quill embroidered sun in the center of it. You tell her to take him for her man!'

" 'We will do so!' the women cried, and started off for the buffalo trap as fast as they could run.

"Old Man hurried back to the waiting men, and hurriedly put on his fine clothes, the ones that he had described to the women.

"Trembling with excitement, and out of breath from their long, swift run, Old Man's messengers arrived at the buffalo trap and told their wonderful news, — that men had come to marry them; that each woman was to choose the man that she thought would best suit her. The butchering of the animals ceased at once, and the women started for their camp to put on their good clothes and recomb their hair. They wanted to appear as neat and clean and well dressed as possible, before the men. Yes, all ran for their camp, all except the chief woman. Said she: 'I cannot leave here until I finish skinning this spotted medicine calf. Go, all of

Old Man and the Woman

you, and I will join you as soon as I can.'

"The work took more time than she thought would be required, and when she arrived in camp with the valuable skin, she found all the other women dressed and impatient to go and choose their men. 'Oh, well, it does n't matter how I look,' she said. 'I am chief; I have a name; I can go choose my man dressed just as I am. How did you say the man chief is dressed?'

"They told her again what he wore, according to what the messenger man had told them, and she said: 'I'll choose him. Chief, I suppose, must mate with chief.'

"And so she went right on with the others, wearing her butchering dress, all stiff with blood and grease from the neck down to the bottom of the skirt; and her moccasins were even more foul than the skirt. Her hands were caked with dried blood, and her hair was not even braided.

"Their chief leading, the women approached the waiting men, all of them standing in a line, and singing a song of greeting. Old Man stood at the head of the line, very straight and proud, and of fine appearance in his beautiful new porcupine-

embroidered clothes. By these the chief
woman recognized him from afar, and said
to herself: 'He is a fine looking man. I hope
that he will prove to be as good of heart as
he is good to look at.' And, leading her
women, she walked straight up to him and
laid a hand on his arm: 'I will take you for
my man,' she told him.;

"But Old Man shrank back, his face plainly
showing his loathing of such a bloody and
greasy, wild-haired woman.

"'I take you for my man,' the woman chief
repeated; and then he broke away from her
hold and ran behind his men: 'No! No! I do
not want you, bloody, greasy woman,' he
cried, and went still farther off behind his men.

"The woman chief turned to her followers
'Go back! Go back to that little hill and there
wait for me,' she told them. And to the men
she said, 'Remain where you are until I return. I shall not be gone long.' And with that
she turned and hurried to her camp. Her
women went to the hill. The men remained
where they were.

"Down at her camp the chief woman took
off her old clothes and bathed in the river.

Old Man and the Woman

Then she put on her fine clothes, a pair of new moccasins, braided her hair, scented herself with sweetgrass, and returned to her women. She was now better dressed than any of them, and they had told Old Man the truth when they said that she was beautiful of face and form: she was the most beautiful woman of them all.

"Again she led her women to the line of waiting men. Again Old Man stood first, stood at the head of them. But she passed him by, as though she did not see him, and he, with a little cry, ran after her, took her by the arm, and said: 'You are the woman for me. I am the chief of the men: you must take me!'

" She turned upon him, and her eyes were like fire. She tore his hand from her arm, and cried 'Never touch me again, good-for-nothing, proud-and-useless man. I would die before I would mate with you.'

"And to her women she said: 'Do not, any of you, take him for your man.' And with that she turned and chose a man. The others then, one by one, took their choice of the men. When all had chosen, there was one woman who had no man; all had been taken except Old Man. She would not have him, and became the second wife of one of the men. The choosing over, all started for the women's camp. Old Man, now very sad-hearted, was for following them; but the chief woman turned and motioned him off. 'Go away. There is no food for you, no place for you in our camp,' she told him; and he went away, crying, by himself.

"And that is what Old Man got for being so proud."

July 30.

We break camp and move northward tomorrow. For the past two days some of us have been riding about on this "Backbone-of-the-World," as the Blackfeet call the Rocky Mountains, and we have ridden our horses where, in former times, nothing but a bird could go. The Park Supervisor and his engineers and miners and sappers have blasted out trails over the highest parts of the range, making it easy and safe for tenderfeet tourists to view the wonders of this sub-Arctic, greater than Alpine range of mountains. One of the most impressive views is from the summit of the trail from Upper Two Medicine

Backbone-of-the-World

Lake to Cutbank River. The Dry Fork Trail, it is called. At its extreme height the trail is along a mountain crest about thirty feet in width. Mr. L. W. Hill graphically described the stretch the other day, when, after crossing it, he said: "On its east side one can spit straight down three thousand feet into a lake, and on the other side cast a stone that will go down much farther than that."

Indeed, the view of the mountains and cliffs and canyons from that height is so grand, so stupendous and impressive, that one cannot find words to describe it all.

On another day we went over Cutbank Pass and down the west side of the range, far enough to get a good view of the Pumpelly Glacier, and see the huge ice blocks break from it and drop from a cliff more than two thousand feet in height. They strike the bottom of the canyon with a reverberating crash that can be heard for miles. Just below this glacier, down Nyack Creek three or four miles, is a fine alkaline spring and clay bed where, in other days, old Tail-Feathers-Coming-over-the-Hill and I were wont to go for bighorn, goats, deer, and elk. All these animals came to it in great numbers, and drank the waters, and ate great wads of the salty mud. We once killed a large grizzly there, whose late autumn coat was as black as that of a black bear.

This afternoon we have had further talk about the naming of these mountains. For a wonder, the topographers have not taken away the original name for the outer mountain on the north side of this Cutbank Valley: we find on the map that it is still White Calf Mountain. It was named for one of the greatest chiefs the Montana Blackfeet ever had. As a young man, fresh from his first war trail, he witnessed the signing of the treaty between his people and the representatives of the United States, at the mouth of the Judith River, in 1855, so he must have been born in 1836 or 1837. As a warrior, his rise to fame was rapid, and many are the stories told of his indomitable bravery in facing the enemy. In later years, because of his great interest in the welfare of his people, he became their head chief. He died in Washington, in 1903, while there on tribal business.

The right names of the other mountains

The Names of the Mountains

walling in this valley are as follows: The un-
named mountain next west from White Calf
Mountain is Ahk´-sap-ah-ki (Generous Woman);
Mount James is Ah´-kow-to-mak-an (Double
Runner); Mount Vorhis is O-nis-tai´-na (Wonderful Chief). The west one of the Twin Buttes
is Little Plume; the east one is O-nis-tai´-mak-
an (Wonderful Runner). And, as I have said,
the outer mountain on the south side of the
valley is Muk-sin-a´ (Angry Woman). All but
the last one were named for old-time great
chiefs and warriors of my people, and we
intend that they shall be so named on the
official maps, even if we have to petition the
House of Representatives and the Senate, in
Washington, to make the change! And you,
my readers, lovers of these grandest mountains of our country, will you not be with us
in this perfectly proper request?

Said Takes-Gun-Ahead to me this afternoon:
"Who are these white men, James, and Vorhis,
for whom the mountains were named? Were
they great warriors, or presidents, or wise men?

I had to confess that I had never heard of them.

"Huh!" he exclaimed. And "Huh!" all the
others, even the women, echoed.

III

KI-NUK´-SI IS-SI-SAK´-TA
(LITTLE RIVER)

August 2.

WE moved over here on Little River — or, as the whites have named it, Milk River — day before yesterday, and made camp at the lower edge of the great body of timber in which the stream has its source. We are here on the Blackfeet Indian Reservation, and several miles from the boundary line of the Glacier National Park. The state game laws do not apply to the reservation, hence we have the right to hunt upon it when and where we please.

Yesterday Takes-Gun-Ahead and I oiled our rifles and started out after meat. We went up the river, passing the old beaver dams that White Fur and Loud Slap built in the long ago, and presently, in the dense growth of pine, cottonwood, and willow, came upon old and fresh picks of deer and elk. We followed

100

Killing a Moose

for a time the trail of four or five elk, and left it to take the very fresh trail of a moose. Takes-Gun-Ahead was in the lead, and within ten minutes he saw the animal not fifty yards away, standing partly concealed behind a clump of willows and watching our approach. Its head was in plain view, and he fired and struck it just at the base of the ear, and it fell, gave a convulsive kick or two, and was dead when we got to it. It was a three-year-old bull, and carried a very ordinary set of antlers, velvet covered and still soft at the points. I dressed the carcass while my companion went back for a horse, and before noon we had real meat — *ni-tap'-i-wak-sin* — in camp. We distributed it among the lodges, and there was great rejoicing. Later in the day Two Guns and Black Bull brought in a fine buck mule deer, and at sunset Big Spring returned with the meat and skin of a yearling ram that he had killed on the outer point of Divide Mountain. It was like old times, — the camp red with meat, — and we all felt rich and happy.

The killing of the moose in this particular place brought out a lot of reminiscences of happenings here on Little River in other days and of them all I think that Takes-Gun-Ahead's story was the best. As the pipe went the first round after our feast of roast moose ribs in Black Bull's lodge, said he: "I will tell you the story of

"OLD MAN AND THE WOLVES

"One day in that long ago time, Old Man was wandering along the edge of this forest, having come over from cutbank way. He was feeling very lonely, and wondering what he could do to have a more lively time, when, as he approached the river here, probably right where we are camped, he saw a band of six wolves sitting on the bank, watching him. He stopped short, watched them for a time, and then approached them, whining out: 'My younger brothers! My younger brothers! I am very lonely! Take pity on me: let me be a wolf with you!'

"As I have said, the wolves were six: the old father and mother, their two daughters, and their sons, Heavy Body and Long Body. The old father wolf answered Old Man. 'Just what do you mean?' he asked. 'Is it that you want me to change you into a wolf

Old Man and the Wolves

— that you want to live just as we do?'

" 'I want to live with you, hunt with you,' he answered, 'but I don't want to be changed wholly into a wolf. Just make my head and neck to look like yours, and put wolf hair on my legs and arms, and that will be about enough of a change. I will keep my body just as it is.'

" 'Very well, we will do that for you,' said the old wolf; and he took a gray medicine and rubbed it on Old Man's head and neck and legs and arms, and made the change. 'There!' said he. 'My work is done. I would like to have made you all wolf, your body as well as the rest of you, but you will do as you are; you are quite wolf-like. And now, let me tell you something about our family. My old wife and I don't hunt much. Your two younger brothers there are the runners and killers, and their sisters help in the way of heading off and confusing the game. Your younger brother there, Long Body, is the swiftest runner, but he has n't the best of wind. However, he generally overtakes and kills whatever he chases. Your other younger brother, Heavy Body, is not a fast runner, but he has great staying power, never gets winded, and in the end brings down his game. And now you know them. Whenever you feel like hunting, one or the other of them, as you choose, will go with you.'

" 'You are very kind to me,' said Old Man. 'I am now very tired, but to-morrow I shall want to hunt with one or the other of them.'

" 'We are also tired; we have come a long way; it is best that we all rest during this night,' said the old wolf; and he led the way up to the top of a high ridge on the north side of the valley, where all lay down.

" 'But why rest out on top of this barren, windy place, instead of in the shelter of the timber?' Old Man asked, his teeth beginning to chatter from the cold.

" 'We never rest in the timber,' the old wolf replied. 'There enemies would have a good chance to take us unawares. Here we can see afar everything that moves, and as one or another of us is always on watch, we can keep out danger. Also, we can look down and see the different kinds of game, and make our plans to chase what we want, head it off, tire it out, and kill it. We always, summer and

Old Man and the Wolves

winter, do our resting and sleeping on high places.'

Before the night was far gone, Old Man became so cold that he trembled all over, and, try as he would, he could not keep his jaws together.

"'You annoy us with your tremblings, and your teeth chatterings; you keep us from sleeping,' the old wolf complained.

"'Well, I shall not annoy you long,' Old Man answered, 'because I shall soon freeze to death!'

"The old wolf aroused his wife and children: 'This tender-bodied elder brother of ours is freezing. I suppose we have to protect him. Lie down in a circle around him and cover him with your tails,' he told them.

"They did so, and he was soon overcome with heat: 'Take your ill-smelling tails from my body; I am wet with perspiration!' he gasped. They removed their tails and he soon began to shiver. 'Put them back! I freeze!' he cried; and they did as he commanded. During the night he had them cover him many times with their tails, and as many times remove them. He passed a miserable night, and so did the wolves, for he kept them from sleeping.

Blackfeet Tales of Glacier National Park

"At break of day all arose, and, looking down into the valley, saw a lone, buck mule deer feeding farther and farther away from the timber. They made a plan for capturing it. They all sneaked around into the timber, and then Long Body and Old Man crept down the valley until the buck saw them and ran, and then they chased it. Long Body soon pulled it down, and Old Man came up in time to seize and break its neck, and felt very proud of himself. The other wolves soon came to the kill, and all feasted. The carcass lasted them two days.

"Again and again they went to the top of the ridge to pass the night, and Old Man soon became so used to the cold that he did not need covering. When the deer was eaten, they killed another one, and then a buffalo bull, which lasted them some days. Then, after two failures in chasing antelope and some hungry days, Long Body killed a big bull elk, just outside the timber here. They were several days eating it, but at last all the meat and the soft bones were finished, and nothing but the backbone and the hard leg bones remained. Said the old wolf then: 'We must be

Old Man and the Wolves

saving of what we left, for it may be some time before we can make another killing. To-day we will take turns chewing the upper bone of a hind leg.'

They gathered in a small circle with one of bones, noses to the center, and the old wolf said to Old Man: 'Now, while this chewing is going on, bone splinters are bound to fly. You must keep your eyes tight shut until it comes your turn to chew, else you may get a splinter that will blind you.'

'Old Man did as he was told. The old wolf began the chewing, and after gnawing off the end of the bone, and getting a little of the marrow, called out to his wife that it was her turn to chew and passed her the bone. And so from one to another it went around the circle until Long Body got it, and Old Man's turn came next. His curiosity now got the better of him: he just had to see what was going on, and slowly opened one eye, the one next to Long Body. All the wolves had their heads to the ground or resting on their fore paws, and all — even Long Body, busily chewing the bone — kept their eyes tight shut. 'Huh! This is a queer way to feast,' Old Man said to himself, and just then a splinter flew from the bone and struck his open eye, not putting it out, but causing him great pain and making him very angry. 'I will pay him for that!' he thought, and waited his turn at the bone, becoming more and more angry as he waited.

" 'Your turn, Old Man,' said Long Body after a time, and passed him the bone. Old Man took it, chewed it for a time, looking sharply at all the wolves. All had their eyes tight shut, so, raising the bone as high as he could, he brought down with all the force of his arm upon Long Body's head and killed him. The other wolves, hearing his twitching, as he died, opened their eyes, saw him dead, and Old Man staring in horror at what he had done.

" 'Oh, what have you done! You have killed younger brother!' the old wolf cried.

" 'I did n't mean to,' Old Man answered.

When he was chewing the bone he let a splinter fly and it struck me in this eye. I meant to punish him a little for being so careless, but I did not mean to kill him. I must have struck harder than I thought to do.'

Old Man and the Wolves

" 'You had your eyes open! It was your fault that you got the splinter!' the old wolf said; and then he and all the rest began grieving for their dead.

"All the rest of that day, and all through the night, they howled and howled, and Old Man thought that he would go mad from the mournfulness of it all. He was very sorry — he hated himself for what he had done in his anger.

"The mourning-time over, the wolves dug a hole in the ground and buried Long Body, and then scolded Old Man. 'Had you killed my son intentionally,' the old wolf concluded, 'we would have had your life in payment for his life. As it is, we will give you one more trial: see that such an accident as that never again occurs!'

" 'Younger brother,' said Old Man, 'I am grieving and very restless because of what I have done. I want to be moving; to be doing something. Let Heavy Body go with me up in this pine forest, and we will try to kill something.'

"The old wolf remained silent for some time, thinking, and at last answered: 'Yes, I will allow him to go with you, and remember this: if anything happens to him, we shall hold you responsible, and great will be your punishment!'

"The two started off, and Old Man said to his partner, 'In some ways I am wiser than you. I have this to say, and you must heed it: Whatever you start after, be it deer or elk or moose, and no matter how close you may get to it, if it crosses a stream, even a little stream that you can jump, stop right there and turn back. Mind, now, even if a few more leaps will get you to the animal's throat, you are not to make those leaps if it crosses a stream. Should you keep on, death in some form will get you.'

"'How do you know this?' Heavy Body asked.

"'I may not tell you all that I know,' Old Man replied. 'I have given you the warning; heed it.'

"'They went farther up in the timber, and after some nosing of trails started a big bull moose, and took after it, Heavy Body running in the lead. He was fast gaining upon it, was almost at its heels, when it jumped into a wide,

Old Man and the Wolves

long pond, really a widening of the creek, and started swimming across it to an island, and from that to the other shore. Heavy Body thought of Old Man's warning, but said to himself: 'He does n't know everything. I must have that moose!' And into the water he went and started swimming toward the island. And just as he was nearing it a water bear sprang from the shore, and killed him, and dragged him to land, and Old Man appeared at the edge of the pond just in time to see the bear and her two nearly grown young begin feasting upon her kill. With a heart full of rage and sorrow, he turned back into the timber and considered how he could revenge the death of Heavy Body.

"Two mornings later, just before daylight, Old Man came again to the shore of the pond, and close to the edge of the water took his stand and gave himself the appearance of an old stump. Soon after sunrise the old water bear, coming out from the brush on the island, saw it, sat up and stared at it, and said to herself: 'I do not remember having seen that stump before. I suspicion that it is Old Man, come to do me harm. I saw him right there when I killed the wolf.'

"She stared and stared at the stump, and at last called out her young, and said to one of them: 'Go across there and bite, and claw that stump. I believe that it is Old Man. If it is, he will cry out and run when you hurt him.'

"The young bear swam across and went up to the stump, and bit, and clawed it, and hurt Old Man. He was almost on the point of giving up and running away, when it left him and went back to the island and told the old one that the stump was a stump, and nothing else. But the old one was not satisfied. She sent the other young one over, and it bit and clawed Old Man harder than its brother had, but he stood the pain, bad as it was, and that young one went back and also said that the stump was just a common old stump and without life.

"But the old water bear was not yet satisfied. She went across herself, and bit and tore at the stump with her claws, and what Old Man had suffered from the others was nothing compared to what he endured from her attack. He stood it, however, and at last, satisfied that her children had been right, that

Old Man and the Wolves

this was a stump and nothing else, she left it and started back for the island. Then it was that, just as she was entering the water, Old Man picked up the bow and arrows he had made during the two days back in the timber and shot an arrow into her, well back in the loin; but she dove under water so quickly that he could not see whether he had hit her or not. She swam under water clear around back of the island, and went ashore where he could not see her. He turned, then, and went away back in the timber, and slept all the rest of the day and all of the following night.

"Early the next morning he was approaching the pond by way of the stream running from it, when he saw a kingfisher sitting on a limb of a tree overhanging the water, and looking intently down into it: 'Little brother, what do you there?' he asked.

"'The old water bear has been shot,' the bird answered. 'She bathes in the water, and clots of blood and pieces of fat escape from the wound, and when they come floating along here I seize them, and eat them.'

"'Ha! So I did hit her!' Old Man said. 'How badly, I wonder?'

Blackfeet Tales of Glacier National Park

"He went on up the shore of the stream, trying to think of some way to get complete revenge for the death of Heavy Body, when he heard some one out in the brush chanting: 'Some one has shot the old water bear! I have doctor the old water bear! Some one has shot old water bear! I have to doctor the old water bear!'

He went out to see who this might be, and found that it was the bull frog, jumping about and making the chant after every jump. He went to him and asked if the bear was much hurt?

"'There is an arrow in her loin,' the frog answered, 'and as soon as I find a certain medicine plant, I shall pull the arrow out and apply the crushed plant to the wound. I believe that I can save her life:'

"'That you never will,' Old Man said, and fired an arrow into him, and killed him. He then took his skin, put it on, tore up a handful of a green plant, and swam to the island. As soon as he reached the shore he began chanting as the frog had done: 'Some one has shot the old water bear! I have to doctor the old water bear!' And chanting and jumping,

Old Man and the Wolves

he followed a trail into the brush and came upon the old bear and her two young. She was lying on her side, breathing heavily, and her eyes were shut. Old Man bent over her, and, firmly grasping the arrow, shoved it in until it pierced her heart, and she gave a kick and died! He then picked up a club and killed the two young. 'There! That ends the water bear family. I was crazy ever to have made her and her husband!' he exclaimed.

"Casting off the frog skin now, he with great difficulty floated the three bears from the island to the shore of the pond. There, a short distance back from it, he found a bowl-shaped depression in the ground. Into this he dragged the carcasses of the bears, after skinning them and taking off all the fat from their meat and insides, and then he tried out the fat and poured the oil over them, completely covering them and filling the depression. He then called the animals. 'All you who would be fat, come bathe in this oil,' he shouted. And on all sides the animals heard and began to come in. The bears — real bears, the grizzly and the black — came first and rolled in the oil, and ever since that time they have been the fattest of all animals. Then came the skunk; next the badger; after him the porcupine, and rolled in the oil and got fat. The beaver came and swam across the oil. All that part of him above water as he swam — his head and the forward part of his back — got no fat, but all the rest his body — his sides, belly, and tail — became extremely fat. Last of all the animals came the rabbit. He did not go into the oil, but, dipping a paw into it, rubbed it upon his back between his shoulders and upon the inside of each leg. That is why he has no fat on other parts of his body.

" 'Well, there!' Old Man exclaimed, after the rabbit had gone. 'I have done some good. I have avenged the death of my wolf partner and have made fat many of my younger brothers!' And with that he started off seeking more adventures.

"Kyi! My story ends."

August 4.

Not for many years, I am sure, have my relatives and friends here been so happy as they are just now. Instead of beef or no meat of any kind, as is generally the case with them

116

New Robe, the Rescuer

when at home, — some die every winter from want of food, — they have now in every lodge real meat; meat of moose and elk and bighorn, and so are living much as they did in the days before the white men overran their country and killed off their game.

A happy heart sharpens one's wits. All day yesterday, as I knew, my two old relatives, Tail-Feathers-Coming-over-the-Hill and Yellow Wolf, were considering what other one of the tribal stories about the Little River country would most please me. I had told them that I could not put them all down — could use only two or three of the most interesting ones. And so, when we all gathered in Yellow Wolf's lodge last evening, and the pipe was lighted and started on the round of our circle, he said that it had been decided that I should have the story of the rescue of a boy from the Crows, and that he would tell it. It was called, he said, the story of

"NEW ROBE, THE RESCUER

"In the long ago, before our forefathers had taken this country from the Crows, they were one summer camping and hunting on the Big

SUN-WOMAN, DAUGHTER OF TAKES-GUN-AHEAD AND WIFE OF STABS-BY-MISTAKE

New Robe, the Rescuer

River of the North.[1] Came the evening of a long, hot day, and a boy of eight or nine winters — Lone Star was his name — failed to return to his parents' lodge. The chiefs ordered the camp crier out, and he went all among the lodges, shouting the news, and asking if any one had seen the boy? None had; so then the chiefs ordered all the men and youths to go out and try to find him. All that moonlit night, and all the next day, they searched the surrounding country, but got no trace of him. Every alighting buzzard was marked down, but in every instance it was found to be feasting upon the remains of game that the hunters had killed. So then, although his body could not be found, most of the people believed that the boy was dead.

His beautiful sister, Red Cloud Woman, and his father, Black Bear, thought otherwise; they believed that he had been stolen by the enemy, and publicly, all through the camp, the two went, the girl vowing that she would marry whoever would find her brother, the old man adding that she had his permission to make the vow.

[1] Ap-ut´-o-sosts O´muk-at-ai (Big River of the North). The Saskatchewan.

Blackfeet Tales of Glacier National Park

"There was in the camp a very poor young man, named New Robe. So poor was he that he had never owned a new robe, nor a new shirt, nor leggins, nor even new mocassins. His father and mother were dead, and always, as far back as he could remember, he had worn nothing but the used clothes the charitable had given him. He had never been to war, had never done anything to make a name for himself, but now he was eager to start in quest of the missing boy. He had long loved the girl, but had never even spoken to her. He now went to her and said: 'Tell no one about it. Just silently pray for me. I am going to travel far in search of your brother.'

"Said the girl: 'This is not a time for me to hide my heart from you. I have watched you, loved you for a very long time. But what could I say. Nothing. Well I knew my people would not allow me to marry one so poor as you. But now there is hope for us; somehow I believe that this trouble is to be the means of bringing us together. And with that she kissed him, and he went quietly out from camp, unobserved by any one, and started southward on his quest.

New Robe, the Rescuer

"Many days later, in the valley of Old Man's River, New Robe came upon an old campground of the enemy — Crows, of course, for that was then their country. From it he found that they had moved south, and he followed their trail, ever along the foot of the mountains, and knew that he was fast overtaking them. At the River-of-Many-Chiefs-Gathering[1] he found live coals in the ashes of their abandoned fireplaces, and so, upon arriving at the top of the ridge overlooking this stream, he was not surprised to see the lodges of the great Crow camp here — right here where we are encamped to night. They were set up in a great circle, and in the center of it was a huge lodge covered with old lodge skins: the Crows were having their medicine lodge ceremonies!

"As soon as night came and before the moon arose, New Robe descended the hill and entered the camp. The people were all of them gathered at the medicine lodge, singing and dancing, and fulfilling their vows to the sun, so he went from one living lodge to another, looking into each for some sign of the missing boy. By the time he had made the

[1] St. Mary's River.

121

round of the lodges of half of the circle it was midnight, and the people were beginning to go home to sleep. He left the camp and went back on the ridge, having found no trace of the one for whom he searched.

"The next night New Robe descended the ridge and searched the lodges of the other half of the circle, and found not what he sought. When he had finished, the people were still gathered at the medicine lodge, and, desperate, and knowing well the great risk that he would incur, he went toward it, and stood at the outer edge of the great crowd and watched the ceremonial dancing of the different warrior clans.

He kept his face partly concealed with his old robe and moved from place to place around the outer circle of the people, and none observed him, so intent were they upon watching the dancers.

"At last, during a quiet interval between dances, he imagined that he heard some one groaning, but, look where he would, he could see no one in distress, nor could he locate the exact place from which the groaning came. It was a light-voiced groaning, such

New Robe, the Rescuer

as a child would make; he felt sure that it came from little Lone Star, somewhere in that great lodge, and in great pain. He left the place, went outside the circle of lodges, and lay down.

"It was long past midnight when the people returned to their lodges. Then, as soon as the camp became quiet, New Robe returned to the medicine lodge, and, listening, heard faint groaning and located it. It came from the top of the center post, where all the sacrifices to the sun were hung. He was sure then that it was no other than Lone Star up there, lashed to the post, a living sacrifice to the sun, and there to die!

"Well he knew that there, within the lodge, were sleeping the women who had vowed to build the great structure in honor of the sun. And there, too, in his secret, walled-off little inner lodge, slept the medicine man whose duty it was to drive back approaching thunderclouds and rain. He had to risk awakening them! He had at least to attempt to rescue the boy! So, casting off his robe, he climbed the outer wall of the lodge, and from it crawled along one of the big long poles that slanted up to the center

123

post. There he found Lone Star, firmly lashed to one of its forks, and so far gone that he could no longer even groan.

"Silently, very carefully, New Robe unwound the lashing, and then, fastening an end of it under the boy's arms, let him down to the ground. He then descended, and found that the boy was so numb that he could not walk. There was but one thing to do then. He took the helpless one upon his back, stole out of the lodge, and started with him across the big campground. Dawn had come. As he was passing the circle of lodges, an early riser, a woman, saw him and with her shrieks aroused all the near-by sleepers. They rushed out, warriors and youths, the women following, and overtook him. He made no resistance. He could have left the boy and made his own escape, but he would not do that. Several old warriors seized him and the boy, and hurried them to the lodge of the head chief, the women and the youths following and crying out that they be killed. Inside the lodge, the chief motioned them to seats, and in signs asked New Robe what he had to say for himself.

" 'I came not to harm you,' New Robe

New Robe, the Rescuer

answered, 'nor to take from you anything that is yours. I came to find this boy, and take him back to his mourning father and mother and sister. And where did I find him! Tied to the center post of your medicine lodge, there to die from want of water and food, a living but dying sacrifice to the sun! That were too cruel a thing to do. I ask you not to put him back there. If he is to die, I die with him. Shoot us, stab us, kill us in anyway you choose, so that our death be quick!'

"The chief gave him no answer to that. He counseled with the other chiefs for a long time, and at last signed to him: 'You are so brave that we shall give you and the boy a chance for your lives. You are to remain here in this lodge to-day, to-night, to-morrow, and the following night. My young men will keep watch on you, so do not attempt to escape. On the morning following your second night here, you are to be given your chance to leave us unharmed. I shall not now tell you what that chance will be.' And then, turning to his men, he gave them certain orders, and they hurried from the lodge.

"During the two days and two nights, New

Blackfeet Tales of Glacier National Park

Robe prayed as he never had before, prayed for strength and courage to succeed in whatever he should be told to do. The people of the lodge treated him and the boy well. They did not want for food, nor anything else that would make for their comfort. Early in the morning the second night, the chief signed to him: 'It is not my fault, nor the fault of my under chiefs, that you have to undergo this trial for your life and that of the boy this day. My people were crying for your lives; they wanted to drag you two out from here and fill your bodies with arrows. I did not want them to do that; my council of chiefs did not want it done; so we counseled together and hit upon a way to give you a chance for your lives. It is not an easy thing that you have to attempt, but I hope you will proceed. And, whatever happens, believe this: I have done the best for you that I could!'

"A little later, soon after the morning meal, the chief signed the two captives to follow him, and led them to the medicine lodge. In front of it were seven fresh buffalo bull heads which a number of men were skinning, and out in front of them, in a great half-circle,

New Robe, the Rescuer

were gathered every man, woman, and child of the Mountain Crow tribe. New Robe wondered what was to be done with the seven buffalo heads; he suspected that they were to be in some way used in his trail for life.

"'Come!' the chief signed, and led him and the boy to the entrance of the medicine lodge. There they stood, the mark of many flashing, angry eyes, and presently the skinners finished their work, and an old chief placed the shining skulls in a line out from the doorway of the lodge, each one of them a long step distant from another.

"Again the head chief made signs to New Robe: 'There is your trial for life,' he said. 'You are to take the boy on your back, and step one to the other of those skulls until you step upon the last one; pass from it to the ground. If you succeed in doing that, you and the boy are free to go to your home, and none of my people shall harm you on your way. But should you slip from a skull, and even so much as touch the ground with your toe, to save your balance, then the warriors standing out there will fall upon you, and kill you both.'

Blackfeet Tales of Glacier National Park

"New Robe looked long at the seven skulls, considering what he should do. Being freshly skinned, he knew that they were very slippery. And then, which would be safest, to step slowly, carefully, from one to another, or make a run across them touching each one quickly, lightly? They were far apart; too far for slow, deliberate stepping; he concluded that the thing to do was to start running from the back of the lodge, and go along the line of them as fast as he could with his burden. He signed to the chief that he would do that, and led the boy to the back of the lodge.

"While going there another thought came to him. He got back of the the boy, and stooped, and while pretending to fix the young one's belt and leggins, kept spitting in two places upon the ground. He then stepped squarely in each pool of the spit and then upon soft ground, and coated his moccasin soles with the sandy earth. Then, suddenly swinging the boy to his back, and running swiftly across the lodge, he lit upon the first skull with his right foot, and went leaping on one from another as fast as he could with the weight upon his back. The third skull began

New Robe, the Rescuer

to turn with him, and he made a weak leap from it, barely alighting upon the next. But it held firm and he made a sure leap from it to the next, and from that to the next, and then, stepping squarely upon the seventh, and last skull, passed from it to the ground, and released the boy from his back.

"The crowd stood silent, sullen, watching him. The head chief came to his side and spoke to them, and they suddenly broke out in loud cheers. The chief then signed to New Robe: 'There is one thing more you are asked to do before we send you home. You do not have to do it, but we hope that you will. Come with me!'

"They went to the lodge of a young chief, and when they were seated, the chief signed to New Robe: 'My father, once a great chief, is an old man. He does not want to die of old age and long and painful illness, and he wants a chance to kill one more enemy before he dies. He wants to fight you. If he kills you, then that will be good. If you kill him, then you shall have his war horse and all his weapons, and I will give you a fine present, and you and the boy shall go to your home in perfect safety. Now, what say you to that?'

" 'I have no weapons,' New Robe objected.

" 'Weapons you shall have,' the other replied. 'All the warriors of the camp are anxious to loan you what they have. You shall go with me and examine what they have until you find just what you want.'

"New Robe considered the matter. If he won out, what honor, what a *coup* it would be to return his people with the weapons and the war horse of his enemy. If he lost, if he was killed — a sudden doubt struck him, and he asked: 'If I fall, what will become of the boy?'

" 'We promise you now,' the chiefs both answered, 'that in that case some of us will take the boy to within sight of the camp of your people, and send him safely to it.'

I take your word for that, and now give me weapons,' said New Robe.

"He was offered his choice of many bows and spears, war clubs and knives, but took only a short, lithe bow and a handful of well-feathered arrows. Then, standing within the circle of the lodges, he awaited the coming of the old chief. He soon appeared, wearing a

New Robe, the Rescuer

beautiful war costume and riding a sorrel pinto war horse. And now, dressed as he was, and easily controlling his fiery-tempered mount, he did not seem to be so very old; at a distance one would have thought him a young warrior. His weapon in hand was long, scalp-tufted spear. On his back he carried a bow and otter-skin quiver of arrows, and in his belt, in a handsome sheath, quill-embroidered was his knife. Said New Robe to himself: 'He looks strong, he is brave. Well, I too must be brave, and watchful.'

"Forth and back across the other side of the big circle rode the old man, singing a war song, brandishing his spear, keeping his prancing war horse well in hand. And then, suddenly urging him forward, he came swift as the wind at New Robe. And he, dropping his tattered wrap, awaited his coming with ready bow. On he came, shouting his war cry, and when quite close New Robe let fly his long and heavy-shafted arrow. It struck the old warrior fair in the ribs. He flinched, the mounting blood choked off his war cry, but on he came, and with a last great effort hurled his spear, and fell from

131

his horse and died, — died without knowing that the weapon had passed high over New Robe's head!

"And then what a shout went up from all the people! Shouts of honor for the old chief who had preferred death in a battle instead of in his lodge, and shouts too for the young man who had so bravely faced him. New robe knew not what to do. He stood looking this way, that way, uncertainly. Then came to him the son of the old dead chief and signed to him to take the horse and the weapons of his enemy, and he did so. Then the young man brought to him another horse, a big and gentle black: 'I said that I would give you something,' he signed, 'and here it is. The boy can ride it home. You may go now, both of you, and go without fear of pursuit: not a man in this camp shall follow you!' And without wasting any time the two mounted the horses and rode northward away from the camp.

"In the Blackfeet camp Lone Star's father and mother grieved more and more for the loss of him, but his sister, Red Cloud Woman, would not believe that he was dead; had somehow faith that he was alive; that New

New Robe, the Rescuer

Robe would find him, and bring him safely home. And at last, when she saw that her father and mother were likely to go mad from grief, she told them that New Robe had gone in search of the boy, and that she would marry him, even if he returned alone. Morning after morning she went up on a butte close to camp and watched the great plain stretching away to the south, and all day long, and often on her couch at night, prayed for the safe return of brother and lover.

"And then, at last, after many, many days of worried watching, she saw two riders coming from the south across the plain, and, sure that they were those she had been praying for, ran to meet them. They were the missing ones. They sprang from their fine horses, and she kissed first her brother and then clung to New Robe: 'I am right now your woman,' she cried, and kissed him again. 'And I am proud to be your woman,' she went on, 'so take me up behind you and we will all ride home!'

"She got up behind him on his prancing war horse, and as they rode in he quickly told her of his adventures, and how, at last, he had fought and killed the old war chief, and for that had been given the two horses and all the weapons and fine war clothes she saw. So it was that, coming into camp, she had the tale of his brave deeds to shout to the people, and they, gathering close around, honored his name and gave him a chief's greeting. Yes, the poor orphan had within the length of one moon become a chief, and had made a mourning father and mother happy. That very night he and Red Cloud Woman were given a lodge of their own, and their happiness was complete."

IV

PUHT-O-MUK-SI-KIM-IKS (THE LAKES INSIDE ST. MARY'S LAKES

August 10.

WE left Little River on the 5th, crossed the big ridge dividing the Arctic and the Atlantic waters, and made camp here on the big prairie at the foot of the Upper St. Mary's Lake.

In the old days this great valley, hemmed in by gigantic mountains, was my favorite hunting ground after the buffalo were exterminated and there was no more sport to be had upon the plains.

Hugh Monroe, or Rising Wolf, was, of course, the first white man to see these most beautiful of all our Northern Rockies lakes; with the Piegan Blackfeet he camped at them in 1816, and long afterward, with his growing family of hardy sons and daughters, this became his favorite hunting and trapping ground. When, in the 1830's, that valiant and much beloved missionary, Father De Smet, S.J., was visiting the various tribes of this Northwest country, Monroe was engaged to take him to a conference with the North Blackfeet, then camping on the Saskatchewan River. *En route* they camped at the foot of the lower of these lakes, and there erected a large wooden cross, and named the two sheets of water, St. Mary's Lakes. Later on, the Stevens expedition named them Chief Mountain Lakes, but that name did not last. Monroe and his brother trappers were all Catholics, and they continued to use the name that the great priest had given them, and on the maps they are St. Mary's Lakes to-day.

During my long friendship with him, Monroe told me many stories of his adventures here in early days. This was his favorite mountain resort on account of the great numbers of moose that inhabited the heavily timbered valley and mountain slopes, and of the great variety and numbers of fur animals that were found here. The valley swarmed with elk and deer; there were countless flocks of bighorn and goats on the mountains, and herds of buffalo everywhere along the lower

Hugh Monroe

lake, and below it; but Monroe liked best of all the flesh of moose, and killed large numbers of them every season that he camped here.

His method of catching wolves was simple and unique. He would build an oblong, pyramidal log pen about eight by sixteen feet at the base, and eight feet in height, the last layer of logs being placed about eighteen inches apart. Easily climbing the slope of this, the wolves would jump down through the narrow aperture at the tope to feed upon the quantities of meat that had been placed inside to decoy them, but they could not jump out. Often, of a morning, the trapper and his sons would find ten or more big wolves imprisoned in the trap, and, powder and ball being very costly, they would kill them with bow and arrows, skin them, and drag the carcasses to the river and cast them into it, then take the hides home and peg them on the ground to dry. In this manner they would often, in the spring, have several hundred wolf pelts to pack in to Fort Benton for sale, and prime pelts sold at five dollars each, in trade. Their catch of beaver, otter, mink, martin, and fisher was also large.

Blackfeet Tales of Glacier National Park

Monroe always camped at the foot of the lower lake, near the outlet, and was there more than once attacked by roving war parties of Assiniboines, Crows, and even the Yanktonais. The horses were kept at night in a strong corral just back of the lodge, and in the daytime were watched by some member of the family while they grazed on the rich prairie grasses. All the family — John and Francois, the sons, Millie and Lizzie, the daughters — and even the mother had guns, flintlocks, and a good supply of powder and ball. Early one morning a large war party was discovered approaching the camp, sneaking from bush to bush, some crawling on all fours through the high grass. Lizzie opened fire upon them and killed her man, and then the fire became general on both sides. But the Monroes, in their trenches surrounding the lodge, had the best of it from the start, and eventually made the enemy retreat with a loss of five of their number. Late the following night the Assiniboines crept in to make another attack, but the Monroes were expecting them, waiting for them, and in the bright moonlight could take fairly accurate aim.

The Rocky Mountain Goat

They again drove them off, with a loss of two more of their number, and that time they kept going. Nothing more was seen of them. But for some days the Monroes did not venture far from their camp.

I first saw the St. Mary's Lakes in October, 1882, in company with Charles Phemmister, James Rutherford, Charles Carter, and Oliver Sanderville, all old plainsmen, good company, and best of hunters. We outfitted for the trip at the Old Agency, on Badger Creek, Blackfeet Reservation, and started northward. There was no trail after leaving the crossing of Little or Milk River, and we struck up country toward the big gap in the mountains, in which we knew the lakes must lie, and that evening camped on the shore of a large prairie lake that was black with ducks. I shot a dozen or more of them as they flew over a long point, and to my surprise and delight found that they were all canvasbacks and redheads, and very fat from feeding upon wild celery beds of the lake. I named the sheet of water Duck Lake.

The next day we made a trail down the long hill, and camped at the foot of the lower lake, close to the outlet. Then began two weeks of most glorious sport. We shot elk, deer, and several grizzlies in the valley, and bighorn on a mountain that I named Flat Top, and combed that mountain from one end to another and on all sides for an animal known to us as the Rocky Mountain ibex. We had seen several skins of them, bought from the Stony Indians by Captain John Healy, of Fort Whoopup and Fort Benton fame, but none of us nor any man of our acquaintance — and we knew every trapper and trader in the country — had ever seen one of the animals alive. Of course we found none, as this sub-Arctic animal, which we later learned is a true antelope, and not an ibex or goat, seldom leaves the high cliff mountains for the outer and lower ones of the range. When, later, we did find them, we in our ignorance named them Rocky Mountain goats, and that is the common name for them to-day, despite the fact that they are antelopes.

On this first visit to the St. Mary's Lakes country I was so impressed by the grandeur of its mountains, the beauty of its many lakes, and its plenitude of game, that thereafter for many years it was, more than anywhere else,

Naming the Mountains

my home. In 1883 I brought out to the lakes a good boat that I had had built for me at Fort Conrad, and with it learned that both lakes were alive with whitefish and Mackinaw, Dolly Varden, and cutthroat trout. During the summer of this year I named Red Eagle Mountain and Red Eagle Lake, after my uncle-in-law, Red Eagle, owner of the Thunder medicine pipe, and one of the most high-minded, gentle-hearted Indians that I ever knew. In the autumn of this year Dr. George Bird Grinnell joined me, and we hunted around the lower lake, and went up Swift Current far enough to see what we thought would possibly prove to be a glacier. We had not then time to learn if our surmise was correct. During our hunt Dr. Grinnell killed a large ram at long range, offhand, with one shot from his old Sharp's rifle, on the mountain next above Flat Top, and I therefore named it Single-Shot Mountain.

In the summer of this year I also named Divide Mountain, because it is the outermost mountain on the Atlantic-Arctic watershed. At the same time I named Kootenai Mountain, also for a very good reason. Some members of that tribe were encamped beside me at the foot of the upper lake. I noticed often that they would ride out of camp at daylight and return at noon or a little later with all the bighorn or goat meat that their horses could carry, and finally I asked them where they went to make their killings so quickly.

"Come with me to-morrow and I will show you something," one of them answered. And the next morning I rode with him up Red Eagle Valley and part way up a mountain, where we tied our horses and went on afoot for a couple of hundred yards. Then, looking down into a *coulée*, we saw a dozen or more bighorn in the bottom of it and killed four of them. They had been eating salty clay and drinking from a salt spring that oozes from the ground there, so I named the place Kootenai Lick, and also gave the mountain the name Kootenai. Thereafter I knew where to go for bighorn when I wanted one.

In 1884 I named Almost-a-Dog Mountain, after one of the few survivors of the Baker massacre, which took place on the Marias River, January 1, 1870. At that time Colonel E. M. Baker, with a couple of companies of

The Baker Massacre

cavalry from Fort Shaw, Montana, was trying to find the camp of Owl Child, a Piegan Blackfoot, and murderer of a settler named Malcolm Clark, and arrest him. By mistake he struck the camp of Heavy Runner and his band of friendly Indians, and, although the chief came running toward him waving his letters of recommendation and his Washington medals, Baker ordered his men to begin firing, and a terrible massacre ensued, the Indians firing not one shot in defense, as about all the able-bodied men were at the time on a buffalo hunt. When the firing was over, two hundred and seventeen old men and women and children lay dead and dying in their lodges and in the camp. The soldiers then shot the wounded, collected the lodges and property of the Indians in great piles, and set fire to them and departed.[1]

In the autumn of 1885 Dr. Grinnell, J. B. Monroe, and I made a trip up Swift Current River, and discovered and roughly measured the big glacier at the head of its middle fork, Dr. Grinnell killing a big ram on the ice while we were traversing it and avoiding its deep crevasses. That evening Monroe and I named

[1]The above is an extract from an affidavit by the late Joseph Kipp, who was Baker's scout and guide at the time.

the glacier in honor of Dr. Grinnell, and also named the mountain to the north of it after him. On the following day we were joined by Lieutenant — now Major — J. H. Beacom, Third Infantry, and he gave my Indian name, Apikuni, to the high mountain between Swift Current and the South Fork of Kennedy Creek. Upon our return to Upper St. Mary's Lake, Dr. Grinnel named Little Chief Mountain, Monroe gave Citadel Mountain its name, and I named Yellow Fish, Goat, Going-to-the-Sun, and Four Bears Mountains. Yellow Fish (O-to-ko´-mi) was an Indian who often hunted with us, and Four Bears (Nis-su´-kyai-yo) was the Blackfeet camp crier, and a most amusing man.

It was in 1886, I believe, that we three, and my old-time friend, William Jackson, one-time scout for General Custer and General Miles, cut a trail to the head of the St. Mary's Valley and discovered the great sheet of ice which we named the Blackfeet Glacier. We at the same time named Gun-Sight Pass, and named the peak just west of the glacier, Mount Jackson. It should be Sik-si-kai´-kwan (Blackfeet Man), Jackson's Indian name. He

GOING-TO-THE-SUN MOUNTAIN

Blackfeet Tales of Glacier National Park

was a grandson of Hugh Monroe, a real plainsman, and one of the bravest men I ever knew.

Going-to-the-Sun has been climbed this day, and a flag has been planted upon its summit, Paul E. Walker, Esq., of Topeka, Kansas. Owing to a high cliff upon its upper shoulder, the mountain has always been considered unclimbable. But after long search, and with no little risk, Mr. Walker finally worked out a way up the wall, and out upon the extreme crest, and was undoubtedly the first man, white or red, ever to stand there. He reports that a magnificent view of the mountains and plains is to be had from the great height.

August 12.

We have more real meat in camp. Yesterday Black Bull went up under the north point of Flat Top Mountain, which is on the Indian Reservation, and killed two fat young rams. I went fishing, and in the first pool of the river below the upper lake, caught several two- and three-pound cutthroat trout. We had a great feast in the evening — roast bighorn ribs, broiled trout, a quantity of blueberries, and so on.

146

The Story of the First Horses

After the feast was over came story-telling time, and we heard this man's and that man's experiences in hunting in this vicinity in other days, Tail-Feathers-Coming-over-the-Hill relating a hard experience that befell him when once wintering here with me. He was chasing a wounded elk on the slope of Single-Shot Mountain, and stepped upon a sharp, snow-covered knot that pierced his foot through and through, and kept him laid up for two months. Yellow Wolf then related an old-time tale, which incidentally gave the reason for naming these two sheets of water the Inside Lakes. He called it, he said, —

"THE STORY OF THE FIRST HORSES

"In that long-ago time when the people had only their great, wolf-like dogs for carrying their belongings, there were two very poor orphans, a brother and sister, in the camp. The boy was very deaf, and because he seemed not to understand what was shouted at him, he was believed to be crazy, and not even the relatives of his dead father and mother cared to have him in their lodges. One would keep him for a time and tell him to go, and then another relative would take him in for a short time, and, getting tired of him, send him on to another lodge. And wherever he went, his beautiful young sister went with him. Often, in good weather, when camp was moved, the two would stay at the old camp-ground, living on cast away meat so long as it lasted, and then they would overtake the camp and go into the nearest lodge, and at least be sure of a meal.

They were generally barefooted and always shabbily dressed. It was a hard life that they led. And because he was so deaf, and believed to be crazy, the boy had not even one playmate in all the camp, nor had his sister, for she knew that it was her duty to be always at his side. There came a time, however, when a childless woman, wife of a great and rich chief, wanted the girl to raise as her own daughter, and after many days the boy persuaded her to be adopted, and he was left alone and more lonely than ever.

"Not long after this separation, the camp moved one day, and the boy, Long Arrow, remained at the old camp-ground to live there as long as he could on the leavings of the people. At last he finished the last scrap of

The Story of the First Horses

thrown away or forgotten meat and started to overtake the camp. The day was hot, terribly hot, but despite that the boy traveled as fast as he could, often running, and perspiration streamed from his body and his breath came short and fast in loud wheezes. Suddenly, while running, he felt something give way with a snap in his left ear, felt something moving out from it, and reaching up he pulled from it a long, round, waxy object that looked like a worm. He held it in his hand and ran on, and noted that with the left ear he could plainly hear his footsteps upon the trail. A little later something snapped in his right ear, and began to move out of it, and he took from it another worm-like substance, and keeping both in his hand, ran on. He could now hear plainly with both ears, and so happy was he that he felt almost as though he could fly.

"But that was not all the good that was to come to him that day. Early in the morning a hunter had left camp with his pack dogs, and had taken the back trail in search of buffalo, and just before the boy appeared he had killed one, and was butchering it when he saw the boy approaching him. This hunter, Heavy Runner, was a chief, and one of the kindest men in the whole camp. He had long thought to do something for this boy, and now, when he saw him coming, he said to himself: 'The time has come. I shall do something for him!'

"The boy came to him and his kill, and he shouted to him, at the same time making signs: 'Sit you down, my boy, and rest. You are wet with sweat, and covered with dust. You must be very tired. Take this piece of tripe and eat it. And now let me tell you something: from this day you are to be my boy. I adopt you. You shall have a place in my lodge; good clothes; a good bed. Try to be good, and deserve it all. I am going to try to make a man of you.'

"'Heavy Runner, your kind words make me want to cry,' said the boy, his voice trembling, tears dropping from his eyes. He swallowed painfully, brushed away the tears, sat up straight, and went on: 'I shall be glad to be your son. I will do all that I can to deserve what you give me. And now, let me tell you something. As I was running away back there on the trail, and breathing hard, first in one

The Story of the First Horses

ear, and then in the other, something broke with a snapping noise and out came these two worm-like things, and at once hearing came to me. I believe that I could hear a mouse walking if he were away out there beyond your kill.'

"'Now, that is good news, and a good sign!' Heavy Runner shouted. He was not yet used to the fact that the boy could hear. Then, remembering, he said more gently: 'You take good rest while I finish butchering this animal and packing the dogs, and then we will each take what meat we can carry and go home. Yes, boy, you have a home now, and a good one.'

"That evening, when Heavy Runner told his woman that he had adopted Long Arrow, she made a great outcry: 'How could you, and without asking me, adopt that deaf, crazy boy?' she asked. And then, she cried, and said that she would not have him for a son, and ran from the lodge. People gathered around and pitied her and said that she was right; that the boy was crazy and deaf and worthless, and would not mind, and as soon as he got good clothes he would urn off and again live at old campgrounds.

"After a time she went back to her lodge, and as soon as she entered it Heavy runner said to her: 'Now, at once, cease your crying, and take the anger from your heart. I have adopted this boy, and he is my boy. He is no longer deaf; he was never crazy. He is a good boy and I shall make a man, a chief of him. See that you treat him well, even if you cannot love him. And believe this: if you do not treat him well, you shall be the one to suffer. To-morrow morning, begin making some good moccasins for him. I, myself, shall cut out his clothes, and he can sew them.'

"So began a new life for Long Arrow. If the woman did not love him, she at least treated him well. He did everything that he could think of to please Heavy Runner. He went hunting with him, and brought home heavy loads of the meat that he killed, and in every possible way was of use to him. And yet he was not satisfied; he kept saying to himself: 'I want to do something great for this man who is so good to me!'

"Time passed. The boy grew up to be a fine young man; good of heart and of fine appearance; and at last Heavy Runner's

The Story of the First Horses

woman loved him as though he were her own son. But in one thing he was very different from the other young men of the camp: he made no close friends, and when not needed by Heavy Runner wandered much by himself. Excepting his sister, whom he frequently took for long walks, he had little to say to any one, and so the people, all but she and his foster parents, continued to believe him crazy.

"One evening he said to Heavy Runner: 'Tell me. What must one do to become a chief?'

" 'One must be very brave, must be fearless when facing the enemy, and of very kind heart; full of pity for the poor and the old and the sick, and always anxious to help them,' the chief replied.

" 'Well, I want to become a chief. What is the first thing for me to do?' he asked.

" 'The first thing to do is to go to some far and dangerous place, and get your medicine. That is, something that will make you favored by the gods, and bring you good luck in battle, and in all matters of life,' Heavy Runner told him.

Blackfeet Tales of Glacier National Park

" 'That I shall do,' said the young man, 'but, first, will you not call in the chiefs, and the medicine men and braves, and let me hear from them where they went, and what they did to get their medicine? I shall then have a better idea of what I am to do.'

" 'We will have in our lodge full of them,' Heavy runner said. And the next morning he shouted out invitations for a smoke, asking only the great of the tribe to come to it. They came, filling the lodge, and then, when the pipe was going the round of the circle, he told why he had invited them to the smoke; asked them to give their experiences in their search for medicines.

"One after another they told their adventures; where they went; what they did; what they saw; what narrow escapes from death they had. And at last it came Spotted Bear's turn. But he refused to give his experience.

" 'What,' he cried, 'tell that crazy youth about my adventure? Why, I wouldn't waste my breath on him!'

" 'But he is a poor boy; he wants to know; you might tell it him in a short way,' pleaded Heavy Runner.

The Story of the First Horses

" 'Well, I will tell it; not for his benefit, for he is crazy, and would not understand; but I will tell it so that you all may know what I did,' the surly one answered.

" 'From this very place I traveled southward along the foot of the mountains. Seven days and seven nights I traveled, stopping only now and then for a short rest and sleeping very little, and on the morning after the seventh night I arrived at the shore of a small lake. There I met a stranger man who asked me what I sought, and I told him that I was wandering in search of a strong, a powerful medicine. "Ah!" said he, "in such a matter I cannot help you. Go on south for three days and three nights, and you will find a man who will give you what you seek."

" 'I went on. Stopping only for short rests, and rarely sleeping, I traveled south for three days and three nights from that place, and in the morning after the third night arrived at a long, wide lake running away back in the mountains. I looked at it, looked at the mountains, turning this way, that way, and when I turned a last time, lo! there in front of me stood a man, fierce of face, dressed in beautiful strange clothing, wrapped in a robe such as I had never seen before, and carrying a spear with a big, flint point.

" " "What do you here?" he asked. "Are you not afraid to come to this, the home of us gods of the deep waters?"

" 'I answered that I was not afraid; that I feared neither gods nor men, nor any animal of the earth, the sky, or the deep waters. And at that he cried out: "You are brave! The brave shall be rewarded! Come with me!"

" 'I went with him to his lodge. I am promised to secrecy; I dare not tell you where it was. He took me in and fed me, and gave me this robe that I am wearing, this medicine robe, and taught me the prayers and ceremony that goes with it. I asked him what kind of a robe it was, and he answered that it was the skin of an elk-dog;[1] an animal as large as an elk, and, like the dog, useful for carrying burdens. The gods, he said, rode them, guided them wherever they wanted to go.

" 'Said I: "May I have one of those elk-dogs to ride home?"

" " "No! They are only for the gods to use,"

[1] Po-no-ka-mi-ta (elk-dog). The horse.

The Story of the First Horses

he answered, and told me to go. I came home.
I have the robe. Here it is, proof of all that I
have told you. Ah! And this crazy youth
would know where I went, what I did! It is
to laugh to think of his going there!'

"The pipe went a last round, and then the
chiefs and medicine men and braves went home.
As soon as they were gone Long Arrow said to
Heavy Runner: 'My chief, you know that I am
not crazy. I feel that I must go on adventure,
and I want to go where Spotted Bear went,
and prove to him that I can go as far and face
as many dangers as he did. Will you let me go,
and keep secret from every one whither I have
gone and for what purpose?'

"'What you propose is just what I want
you to do,' Heavy Runner answered. 'You
shall start to-morrow, taking with you all the
moccasins and other things you will need, and
your foster mother and I will tell no one anything about you.'

"At break of day the next morning, while
all the people of the great camp still slept,
Long Arrow started on his journey of discovery. Straight south he went, by day and by
night, resting and sleeping at long intervals,

and then only for a very short time. On the third day he arrived at the small lake that Spotted Bear had mentioned, and there met the man of that place, even as he had done.

" 'What seek you?' the man asked.

" 'Knowledge! Medicine! The way to become a chief!' Long Arrow answered.

" 'I cannot help you. Go on south for seven days and seven nights, and you will come to a great lake, and there you will meet a man who can help you if he cares to do so. It may be that he will not even show himself to you, but anyhow it is worth your while to go there and try to meet him.'

"Long Arrow went on for seven days and seven nights, resting and sleeping less than ever, eating nothing except now and then a piece of dry meat not so large as his hand. Early in the morning after the seventh night, exhausted, hardly able to drag one foot after the other, he came to the great lake, and some distance back from its shore fell down on the grass and fell into a sound sleep. It was late afternoon when he awoke, and, opening his eyes, he was surprised to see a boy standing beside him. He was a beautiful child, by far

The Story of the First Horses

the most perfect of form and feature that Long Arrow had ever seen; so beautiful that it did not seem possible he could be of this earth, a child of the people of this earth.

"Said the boy to him: 'I have been waiting here a long time for you to awake. My father invites you to his home.'

"'I shall be glad to visit him,' Long Arrow answered, and sprang up, put on his weapons, and was ready.

"The boy led him straight to the shore of the lake, and there cried out: 'Do not be afraid, follow me!' And having said that, changed into a snipe, entered the water and disappeared.

"Long Arrow was afraid, terribly afraid of the deep, dark water, and the mystery of a place, where a child could suddenly become a snipe. But he said to himself: 'If I fail in my search for a medicine it shall be through no fault of mine,' and he entered the water. Lo! it did not wet him; did not touch him. It parted before him and he went on down the sloping, sandy bottom of the lake, and soon saw, close ahead, a large, fine lodge, on which were painted in red and black the figures of two strange animals.

Blackfeet Tales of Glacier National Park

The boy, arrived at the doorway of the lodge, changed suddenly from a snipe back to his natural self, and cried out: 'Follow me! Here you will be welcome,' and went in. Long Arrow, following him, found himself facing a fine-looking man at the back of the lodge. He was sitting cross-legged on his couch, and wore a beautiful black robe which entirely covered his legs and feet. 'You are welcome here, my son, be seated,' said the man, and told his wife to prepare food for his guest.

"Long Arrow looked about him. On all sides the lodge was hung with beautiful shields, war clothes, weapons, handsomely painted and fringed pouches of sacred medicines, and a porcupine-quill embroidered belt of such brilliant colors that it shamed the rainbow.

"The woman of the lodge soon set food before Long Arrow, and, having long fasted, he ate largely. The man then filled and lighted a pipe, passed it to his guest, and said: 'I knew that you were coming, and I wondered if you would have the courage to follow my son from the shore of this lake down here to my lodge. Not long ago a man of your people came here, but he was afraid; he would not

The Story of the First Horses

follow my son. And there he made a great mistake. I was going to give him the most valuable present ever given by gods to men. As it was, I went out to him where he sat far back from the shore, and gave him the tanned hide of an elk-dog, and sent him home.

He was not worthy of a better present. But you are different. I shall give you something of great value. Remain here with us a few days. My son shall show you my band of elk-dogs; you shall hunt and kill meat for us; and when you go, then you shall have the great present.'

"The boy went out with Long Arrow and showed him the elk dogs. They came running from the timber out upon the open prairie at the foot of the lake, and were a wonderful sight. "They were far larger than an elk, of shining black color, had tails of long hair, and there was long hair all along the top of their necks and hanging down their foreheads from between their restless ears. They were of all sizes, from suckling young to old males and females, and all were very fat and playful, even the oldest of them.

" 'Young man of the earth,' said the boy, 'if you are wise and watchful, these animals and my father's black robe and his many-colored belt may be your present: the three go together. You have noticed that my father always keeps his feet covered with the black robe; that when he arises and goes out of the lodge he is very careful to keep the robe lowered around him, like a dragging woman's dress, so that his feet cannot be seen. Well, you have but to see those feet, and anything that you ask for will be yours.'

" 'I shall do my best to see those feet,' said Long Arrow.

"Several days passed. The old people of the lodge were very kind to Long Arrow, and he in turn did his best to please them, hunting most all of the time and bringing in much meat. And what time he was not hunting, he would sit close to the herd of beautiful elk-dogs and watch them feed and play. When in the lodge he watched closely for a sight of the old man's feet, but he ever kept them closely covered.

"At last, one evening, the old man started to go out of the lodge, keeping his robe well down upon the ground about him, but as he stepped over the low front of the doorway his right knee raised the robe and Long Arrow

The Story of the First Horses

saw his left foot; and lo! it was not a human foot: it was the hoof, the round, hard hoof of an elk-dog! He gave a cry of surprise at the sight, and the old man, realizing what had happened, exclaimed 'Hai-yo! How careless of me! Well, it cannot be helped, it must have been fated that he should see it!'

"He went on out, and upon returning took no pains to conceal his feet: both of them and the ankles were those of the elk-dog.

" 'Well, you have seen my feet, so you can now tell me what I shall give you,' said the old man, as he resumed his seat.

" 'Now, don't hesitate; speak right out; ask for the three things,' whispered the boy.

"And Long Arrow, taking courage, answered 'Give me three things: your black robe, your many-colored belt, and your elk-dogs.'

" 'Ha! You ask a great deal,' the old man cried, 'but, because you are brave and good-hearted and not lazy, you shall have the robe and the belt and a part of my band of elk-dogs. The robe and the belt are the elk-dog medicine. Without them you could never catch and use the animals. There are many prayers and songs and a long ceremony that go with them, and I have to teach it all to you. When you have thoroughly learned them, then you shall go home with your presents.'

"Long Arrow was many evenings learning them all, but at last he could repeat every one of them perfectly, and dance the dances as well as the old man himself, and finally the latter told him one evening: —

"'You have done well. I am glad that my elk-dogs and my medicines are to be in your hands. You may start for home to-morrow. And now, listen! Take good heed of what I am about to tell you.

"'When you leave here, wearing the black robe and the belt, you are to travel for three days and three nights and never once look back.

When you rest, you are to face the north. Be sure, now, that, traveling or resting, you never once look back. The elk-dogs will not at first follow you, but on the third day of your homeward journey you will hear them coming behind you. Even then you must not look back, but keep on walking. After a time they will come on right beside you, and with

The Story of the First Horses

a rope that I shall give you, you will catch one of them and mount and ride it, and all the others will follow you. They will always do that so long as you have the black robe. Lose that, and you lose your animals; they will become wild, and you will never be able to catch and train them.'

" 'As you say, so shall I do,' Long Arrow answered.

"And early the next morning the old man gave him the robe, the belt, and a rope made from the head hair of buffalo bulls, and he started for home, keeping ever in mind and obeying carefully the old man's instructions. At times he had his doubts of the old man. Perhaps a big joke was being played upon him; the elk-dogs would not come on the third day, nor any other day! But he would soon cast off such thoughts, and go on with renewed faith that all would be well with him.

"And on the third day he heard behind him the thunder of many hard hoofs upon the hard plain; the occasional whinnying that he had learned to love so well! And then, an old female leading them, the elk-dogs came close up beside him, and he caught and mounted one of them, and rode on. How happy he was! He realized what this would mean for himself and for the people. These elk-dogs would rapidly increase in number; there would soon be enough of them for all the people, and then they would ride instead of walk, and their lodges and all their belongings would be carried by the animals. 'And now I can do something for those who have been so good to me,' he said to himself, and rode on, singing the new songs that he had learned.

"It was late in the afternoon on the day that he approached the camp. All the men had returned from the hunt; every one was outside the lodges, resting in the warm sunshine. The first to discover him gave a shout of surprise and alarm. All the people sprang up and stood gazing at the strange sight. They asked one another what the strange big black animals could be? And was it really a man sitting astride one of them?

"'It is some fierce god bringing his fierce animals to destroy us,' shouted Spotted Bear, the very man who had so contemptuously

The Story of the First Horses

used Long Arrow, who had not had the courage to follow the boy-snipe into the water. Again he cried out: 'Surely it is an evil one coming to destroy us.' And he fled, and all the people fled with him and took to the brush.

"Long Arrow rode into camp and dismounted at Heavy Runner's lodge, and all the elk-dogs came up and crowded around him and the one of them that he had been riding. 'Heavy Runner! Heavy Runner!' he shouted. 'Be not afraid! I am only your son, come back to you!'

"Heavy Runner heard the well-known voice and was no longer afraid. He came hurrying from the brush, all the people following him, and they all crowded around Long Arrow and his strange animals. Said the youth then: 'Only father and mother that I ever knew, I have brought to you, excepting one female and one male, all these strange and useful animals. As you see, they can be ridden; you will no longer have to walk. Also, they will carry for you everything that is yours. I am glad that I can give them to you, both of you who have been so good to me.'

"'How generous of you!' Heavy Runner

cried. But his wife could say nothing: she embraced Long Arrow and wept.

"'Where did you get the strange black ones?' a chief asked.

" 'I will tell you all about it this evening; I am cautioned not to talk about the gods in the daytime,' Long Arrow answered. And after picketing the animal he had ridden on good grass, and driving the others out from camp, he went into the lodge and rested.

"That evening all the chiefs and warriors came into the lodge, Spotted Bear with them, and he told all about his strange adventures, of his life with the Under-Water People, and how the old man had given him the elk-dogs, and the black robe and the belt that he wore. And, of course, he told about Spotted Bear's cowardice in failing to follow the boy-snipe into the water, and he fled from the lodge, and his chieftainship dropped from him as he fled. Ever afterward he was no more than a woman in that great camp; never again was he allowed to sit with the chiefs and warriors! And when Long Arrow had finished telling them all about his wonderful adventures, the chief cried out: 'We will move camp to that

The Story of the First Horses

lake of the Under-Water People. They have more elk-dogs; we will ask for them, give anything to obtain possession of such valuable animals.'

"They moved south to the lake, but, search as they would, could find no elk-dogs, nor did the boy-snipe nor any of the Under-Water People appear, although the medicine men made sacrifice to them and prayed them to show themselves. They did discover, however, that above this lake was another and a longer one, hemmed in by still higher mountains, and so they named the two the Inside Lakes, and that is the name they bear to this day."

August 12.

Last night we all gathered in Stabs-by-Mistake's lodge, and, while the pipe was filled and refilled, and passed from hand to hand on many rounds, we had more tales, strange and weird, of the people of the ancient days. One that our host told especially interested me, and here it is, literally translated for your perusal. It was the story, he said, of

Blackfeet Tales of Glacier National Park

"ONE HORN, SHAMER OF CROWS

"It was in the long ago time, when all three of our tribes, the Blackfeet proper, the Bloods, and we, the Pikun´i, whom the whites mistakenly call Blackfeet, were still living in the North country. The camp of the Pikun´i was on Big River, close up to the foot of the mountains. One of the great chiefs of the tribe was One Horn. Very brave he was, and very rich, for his band of horses numbered more than a hundred head. He had two wives, sisters, but no children. Many orphans called him father, for he had poor old couples care for them, and kept them all well supplied with meat and with skins for clothing. He was a peculiar man, was One Horn. He seldom visited in other lodges, and was a man of few words; it was always difficult to get him to tell of his brave deeds.

"One summer night One Horn had an uneasy dream about his horses, and with the first faint light of coming day arose, washed and dressed himself, and took up his weapons and went out to see if his herd was anywhere in sight. He climbed to a little rise on the edge of the plain, saw them quietly feeding at a distance,

One Horn, Shamer of Crows

and then saw something else: two men asleep in a *coulée* close under the little rise. They were, he thought, young men of the camp, watchers of the horse herds, and he concluded to surprise them and scold them for sleeping when they should be watching the plains for the approach of enemies. More from habit than anything else, he drew his bow, fitted a war arrow to it, and then, creeping close to the sleeping ones, shouted: 'Awake! You lazy ones, awake!'

"To his great surprise they were two enemies, who sprang up at the sound of his voice, and he shot one of them in the breast, and he fell, and as the other turned and ran, he fired an arrow at him and struck him in the back, but he kept on running, the arrow dangling and swaying from his back, and he soon disappeared in the thick brush bordering the river. One Horn went back to camp and sent the warriors out to look for the wounded man, but they never found him.

"Although a very brave warrior, One Horn's voice was always for peace. He thought much about the wars of tribe against tribe and the great loss of lives they caused, and wished that he could put an end to it all. He counted up the different tribes with whom his people were at war — the Sioux, the Assiniboines, Cheyennes, Pawnees, Snakes, Bannocks, Pend d'Oreilles, Flatheads, Nez Percés, Kootenai, and Crows. And the worst of them all were the Crows. He determined to go to the Crows and try to make peace between them and his people.

"Another thought came to him: It was best to say nothing to his people about his plan, for many would make serious objection to it. If he succeeded, they should know all about it upon his return. If he failed, he would never tell them where he had been. So, one evening, he gave his women orders what to do, and kept his horses close in around his lodge. Late that night, when all the camp was asleep, down came the lodge, the pack and travois horses were quietly loaded, and he and his women headed southward, he driving his big herd in the lead. The next morning the people found that they had a mystery that they could not solve: One Horn was gone with all his belongings, gone without telling them one word of his intentions! Why had he left them so secretly, and whither had he gone? They never ceased talking about it and wishing that he would return; they felt safe when he was at their backs.

"Traveling south day after day along the foot of the mountains, One Horn and his women at last struck the River-of-Many-Chiefs-Gathering, and, following it up, came in sight of the prairies at the foot of the lower Inside Lakes. It was then dusk, but not so dark but what they could see that there was a big camp of people at the edge of the timber bordering the lake shore. Said One Horn, 'They must be the ones I seek, the Mountain Crows. As soon as they sleep, we will go on and put up our lodge near theirs.'

"Early the next morning an old man stepped out from his lodge, and saw a strange lodge standing by itself just outside the circle of the big camp. He looked at it a long time, and the growing light at last enabled him to see that there were two huge bears painted on its new white leather skin. He turned and hurried to the lodge of the head chief of the camp, aroused him, and cried: 'Here is a mystery; something to be looked into: just outside the circle of our camp a strange lodge is standing.

Blackfeet Tales of Glacier National Park

It belongs not to us Mountain Crows, nor to our brothers, the River Crows. I know that, for it has painted upon it two big bears, and neither of our tribes has that medicine.'

"The chief hurried to get up and dress, and so did others, and they soon left their lodges and approached the strange lodge. There was a fire within it. Voices were heard in low-toned conversation. Close around a few horses were picketed, and farther out grazed a large band of them, mostly grays and blacks. It was evident that the owner of the lodge was a chief, a bear medicine man, a very rich man. The Crow chief thrust aside the door cutain of the lodge, and entered, the other following. A fine-appearing man at the back of it gave them the sign for welcome, and motioned them where to sit. He lifted a big filled pipe and lighted it, and passed it. The Crow chief smoked first, and then one by one those with him.

"Having passed on the pipe, the Crow chief signed to the stranger: 'You are a Blackfoot?'

"'Yes, I am a Blackfoot,' One Horn answered. 'You are wondering why I, an enemy, have come here and set up my lodge

174

One Horn, Shamer of Crows

beside you. You shall know! I have come to try to make peace between your people and my people. I am tired of all this war, and its wasting of men's lives, and making women and children mourn.'

"'You say well. Your talk deserves attention. Peace between us would be good for us both. I will talk to my people about it,' said the Crow chief.

"And just then One Horn's women set before him and the other Crows dishes of rich berry pemmican, the best of dried meat and back fat, and they ate with the outside chief. Then they smoked again and went home, the Crow chief saying that he would soon give a call for a council, and would send for the Blackfoot to join in it.

"It was not until near sunset, however, that a youth came to invite One Horn to the Crow chief's lodge. He found assembled there all the head men of the tribe, and the chief told him that, after long talk, they had decided that they, too, were tired of war, and would be glad to make peace with the Blackfeet.

"'But be not in a hurry to return home,' the Crow chief concluded. 'Make us a long visit, and during it we will decide together where and when our two tribes shall meet to make this lasting peace treaty.'

"Answered One Horn: 'I shall be glad to camp here with you for the rest of this moon.' And all those present signed to him: 'Yes. Remain here with us for a time.'

"One Horn and the Crow chief became friends. They hunted together, visited often in each other's lodge, and together were invited to other lodges to feast and smoke, and join in the warriors' tales of raids and battles and adventures along far trails.

"The River Crows were at this time en-camped just over the ridge from the Inside Lakes, on Little River, and some of them came frequently to visit their Mountain broth-ers at the foot of the lakes. Among others came a man who was always counting his *coups*. In a gathering of the warriors he would wait until all had told what they had done in war against their enemies, and then he would count one *coup*, only one, that was far greater than any of theirs.

"On a day when One Horn was visiting in the Crow chief's lodge, this man was one of

One Horn, Shamer of Crows

the guests. The talk was of war, and after many there had told what they had done, he said that, with a friend, he was approaching the Blackfeet camp, and they were discovered and surrounded by all the warriors of the tribe. His friend soon fell, as full of arrows as a porcupine is full of quills, but that he, charging this way, that way, shooting arrows fast and killing many Blackfeet, made them give way before him and he escaped from them, although wounded In tho back. Later on, when safe from pursuit, he had drawn out the arrow, and still had it, proof enough of the truth of his tale.

"This man then turned to One Horn, and said, by signs, of course, 'We have all of us here told about our fights, and now it is your turn: tell of your brave deeds.'

" 'I have nothing to say that will interest you; mine have been just the common experiences of those who go on raids. No, I have nothing to say,' he answered.

" 'But you must tell us one great thing that you have done,' the River Crow insisted.

"And again One Horn answered: 'What I

have done would not interest you. I have nothing to say.'

"The man then turned to the Mountain Crow chief and said: 'This is a poor kind of a friend for you to have! He has done nothing; he is no chief, he is a woman!'

"'I do not know for sure, but I think that he is a chief, that he has a big war record,' the host answered him.

"And then the guests went their several ways, the River Crow laughing shrilly, contemptuously, as he left the lodge.

"It was not long after this that the River Crow came over again from Little River, and again was one of a party of guests in the lodge of the chief of the Mountain Crows. Once more the talk was of war, and when it came this man's turn to talk, he drew an arrow from his quiver, laid it on the ground in front of him, and said: 'There! No one here, nor in the camp of the Mountain Crows and the camp of the River Crows, has ever equaled what that stands for. That is the arrow that I drew from my back after my partner was killed, and I fought my way single-handed through the hundreds of Blackfeet warriors,

One Horn, Shamer of Crows

killing many of them, and so frightening them that they dared not pursue me.'

"One Horn leaned over, looked at the arrow, and gave an exclamation of disgust: 'That is my arrow,' he signed. 'I know this man now. At dawn, one morning, I discovered him and his partner asleep near our camp. I crept up to them and shouted, thinking that they were our horse-herd watchers, and when they sprang up, I saw that they were enemies. I shot one of them dead. This man turned and ran, never even firing at me, and I shot an arrow into his back, but he kept on going and escaped from me in the brush! Yes. That is the very arrow I shot into him!'

"'It is a lie! A big lie!' the River Crow said, and signed.

"For answer to that, One Horn went to the door of the lodge and shouted to his women to bring over his quiver of arrows. It was soon handed in to him, and he said: 'I have here two kinds of arrows: hunting arrows and war arrows. Here are the war arrows.' And he laid them beside the arrow in front of the boaster. All there saw at once that they were exactly like it in every way, had the same private mark just back of the point. And suddenly, with jeers and cries of 'Liar!' 'Coward!' they took handfuls of ashes and earth from the fireplace and threw them in the River Crow's face and on his head, and he ran for the door and was gone, leaving the arrow behind. One Horn picked it up and put it in his quiver, and said: 'That no doubt ends his lying bragging!'

"Some days after this exposure of his lying, the River Crow, watching his chance, entered the lodge of the Mountain Crow chief and said to him: 'That Blackfoot has shamed me. I was a chief, but now all people laugh at me. I want revenge. Let me kill that friend of yours and I will give you three of my best horses!'

" 'What you ask is impossible!' the chief replied. 'He is my friend! We have smoked together, have eaten together. I cannot allow you to kill him. And for your lying you deserve what you got!'

"The River Crow sneaked away, but on the next evening, when none but the chief and his women were at home, he came again. And this time he said: 'Let me do what I want to do; you know what that is; and I will give

One Horn, Shamer of Crows

you five of my best horses and my beautiful young daughter.'

"And this time the chief did not give him a short answer. He thought over the offer for a long time. He knew that it would be a terrible thing to betray his Blackfoot friend, but the temptation was great. His women were getting old. He wanted that beautiful girl. And at last he gave way to the temptation: 'It shall be as you wish,' he told the man. 'All is arranged for to-morrow; we go with the hunters on a big buffalo hunt and there will be no chance for you to do what you want to do. Come the day after to-morrow and I will help you — if you need my help — to kill the Blackfoot.'

"Very early the next morning the hunters started out after buffalo, One Horn taking with him one of his women to help in the butchering and packing in of the meat. They were no sooner gone than one of the Crow chief's women hurried to One Horn's lodge and told his other woman all about the plan to kill him. She told it because she was jealous; she did not want her man to take another wife!

Blackfeet Tales of Glacier National Park

"So it was that, when One Horn came home that evening, this wife ran to him and embraced and kissed him as though she would never let him out of her arms. This strong showing of love was unusual with her, and he asked her the cause for it.

" 'Because to-morrow you are to die, and sister and I are to become slaves. See now what you have done by coming to try to make peace with these Crows! And she told him all about the plot to end his life.

"But One Horn just laughed: 'Wipe away your tears and take courage,' he told her. 'These Crows will not kill me, a bear medicine man, and a chief. They cannot kill me. I will show you to-morrow something that will surprise you!'

"That night he kept his favorite war horse picketed close to his lodge, and the next morning he carefully dressed himself in his beautiful war clothes, painted himself and his horse, took his bow and arrows, his shield and spear, and rode into the center of the big camp, and called upon the Crow chief to come out. He did come out, also dressed for battle, and One Horn cried out to him, at the same time making

One Horn, Shamer of Crows

signs, so that he would be sure to understand, 'Your plot is discovered. So you and that River Crow are going to kill me. Where is he? Call him. I want to fight you both. I am a bear. I fight like a bear. Come! Hurry! Let us fight. Ha! I am going to fight my true friend, the chief of the Mountain Crows, he who smoked and ate with me, he who was going to join me in making a lasting peace between our two tribes. Come! Let us fight! Shall it be on horseback or afoot? I give you the choice.'

"The Crow chief gave him no answer. Some of the people, looking on, were beginning to show their anger and shame at his betrayal of a friend. He turned and went back into his lodge, and would not come out again.

"While this was going on, several men had hurried to the River Crow man, stopping in the far end of camp: 'Your plan to kill the Blackfoot is discovered, and he is dressed and armed and mounted, waiting to fight you. He is like a raging grizzly, and his, you know, is the bear medicine. What are you going to do?'

"The man did not answer them. He mounted his horse, and, hidden from One

Horn's sight by the lodges, struck out for the River Crow camp on Little River, and fear was with him. He often looked back to see if he were being pursued by this dreadful bear medicine man who had once wounded him, and was now so anxious to meet him face to face.

"One Horn rode back to his lodge. 'Take down the lodge, pack up everything. We will not stay another day with these treacherous Crows,' he told them, and rounded up and caught what horses were needed for packing and riding.

"Just before they were ready to leave, the Crow chief sent one of his women to say to One Horn that he was sorry for what he had done, very sorry that he had ever listened to the River Crow, and wanted to make reparation. He wanted to give his Blackfoot friend ten head of horses.

" 'Tell him that I will not accept anything from him,' One Horn answered the woman. And he and his outfit started for the north and were soon out of sight of the Crow camp.

"Some days afterward they arrived at the camp of their people on the Big River of the

The Elk Medicine Ceremony

North, and had no sooner set up their lodge than One Horn called a council of the chiefs and told them where he had been and for what purpose. " 'Although I accomplished nothing, I am glad I went,' he told them. 'I now know the Crows. They are liars all, and not to be trusted. I advise that we begin a steady war against them.'

"The other chiefs agreed to that. Messengers were sent to the brother tribes, the Bloods and the North Blackfeet, and to the Gros Ventres, friends of the Blackfeet, and the war was started. Little by little, summer after summer, they drove the Crows southward, killing many of them, and were not satisfied until they forced them to the country south of the Elk River,[1] where they have ever since remained. So, because of their treachery, the Crows lost a great and rich country."

THE ELK MEDICINE CEREMONY

August 18.

Not in many, many years have I been so affected as I was this morning. For some days I have had a high fever, and have slept but little at night. In-si-mak´-i (Growth Woman), Yellow Wolf's wife, had been doctoring me with the good old remedy for fevers, sweet

---

[1] Po-no-ka´-is-i-sak-ta. Elk River; the Yellowstone River.

sage tea, but it seemed to have no effect. So Tail-Feathers-Coming-over-the-Hill announced that he would have his Elk Medicine ceremony for my benefit, and that he was sure that it would cure me of my illness. We had it this morning, and to-night I have a normal pulse and the fever has left me. I will not go so far as to say that it was his prayers that cured me, — prayers far better, far more earnest than those of any Christian preacher I ever heard, — but yet, I am well! To me, all religions are nothing more than the codified superstitions of the ages, but of them all, Christian and pagan, I like best the faith of these, my people, faith that the sun is the conservator of all life and the orderly ruler of this, our earth. And what absolute faith they have in their Sun-religion! Should Christians live as closely to their beliefs as the Blackfeet do to the laws of conduct given them by their Sun god, what a different, what a happy world this would be!

Before I relate the details of the ceremony, I must tell something of the medicine itself.

The Blackfeet believe that, when they lie down and sleep, their shadows, or, as we say,

The Elk Medicine Ceremony

their souls, their spiritualities, leave the body and go on far adventure. Their name for this is Ni-pup´-o-kan (my dream; my vision); and when they awake they really believe that they have experienced all the incidents of their dream, and relate them as having been of actual fact.

When men and animals were first created, they had a common language, and the latter had the power to change themselves at will into the form of man. It was in that long ago time that a man seeking knowledge, and praying earnestly for it, was in his vision visited by an elk in the form of a man, whose name was Po-no-kai´-ût-sin-in-ah (Elk-Tongue Chief).

"I have heard you praying, asking for help. What is it you want? Perhaps I can help you," the elk man said.

The man answered: "I seek some way to relieve my people from sickness; some way to give them long life and happiness. Help me if you can do so."

The elk man answered: "I can help you; I will help you. Through what was given me in my vision I am in great favor with the sun, and all the gods of the earth, the deep waters, and the blue above. That medicine you shall have. I give it to you now!" And having said that, he gave the man a painted lodge, a medicine pipe-stem, beautifully decorated with a down-hanging set of tail feathers of the sage hen, and wound with strips of the fur of the bear and various water animals. And with it, wrapped in clean buckskins, were the skins of birds and animals, all those that live upon the water and in the water, and feed upon the life in the water, fish, and all the various water insects. And having given the man all this, he taught him how to use it, with all the prayers and ceremonies that go with it. The man took all this to his home, and used it, and found that it was great medicine, and ever since that time the Elk Medicine Lodge and the things that go with it have been handed down from generation to generation, to this day.

So now we come to the ceremony that was given to-day for the curing of my illness. It was my lucky day! Early in the morning Mr. Herford T. Cowling, chief photographer for the United States Reclamation Service, arrived at the Great Northern Railway Company's

The Elk Medicine Ceremony

St. Mary's Camp and I went to him and asked if he would take moving pictures of the ceremony, provided the Indians were willing to have him do it. He enthusiastically replied that he would be very glad to take it all in with his crank-machine, so I went to my people to ask if they would permit it to be done. They objected, saying that the ceremony was so sacred that even the presence of white people, antagonistic all of them to their religion, would profane it. They did not count me. I was one of them!

Said I: "Listen, my relatives, and brothers all! We are all soon to die, and as we pass away the whole of the old life goes with us.
Your children, taken away from you by the whites, put in school and taught the white men's religion and manner of living, will know nothing about the way their fathers lived unless I put it all down in writing for all time to come. That I am doing. And how much more interesting it will be if I can have pictures to go with it! Say yes! Let us have, with this that you are to do to-day, the living pictures of it all!"

There followed a long silence, all considering my request. Finally, my best of friends,

Blackfeet Tales of Glacier National Park

Tail-Feathers-Coming-over-the-Hill, wiped tears from his eyes, and said, brokenly: "Ap-i-kun´-i is right. The whites take our children from us and teach them false beliefs. But they teach them to read, and it may be, that, after we have all gone on to the Sand Hills,[1] they will read our brother's writings and see us as we were, making our prayers to the gods, and, having read and seen the pictures of it all, return to the one true faith. I say, let the picture man come!"

"Ai! Ai! Let him come!" all cried, and I sent a messenger for him.

During the ceremony he took six hundred feet of it, and so for all time to come is preserved the interesting ceremony of the Elk Medicine.

The ceremony is always given in a closed lodge, but this time we threw the front of it wide open, so that the lens of that moving-picture machine could take it all in.

As I have said, Tail-Feathers-Coming-over-the-Hill is old, feeble, half-blind, and is himself unable to go through parts of the ceremony. So, on the evening before this came off, he sent for Chief Crow and his wife,

[1] The Sand Hills (Spät-si-kwo). The drear after-life abode of the Blackfeet. Their shadows there had a cold, cheerless imitation of life. 190

The Elk Medicine Ceremony

living near, to help him out. Chief Crow is also a medicine man, his wife, of course, a medicine woman, and he owns the Seizer's medicine pipe. Four other medicine men were there, all of them taking part in the ceremony. In each of the three tribes of the Blackfeet there is a secret society of the medicine men, and the members help one another in their ceremonies, and they and they only can dance with the sacred symbols of their rites.

When I went into the lodge the sacred medicines were hanging directly over the owner's couch, opposite the doorway. They were the sacred pipestem and many skins of water animals and birds enclosed in various wrappings, and a buffalo rawhide painted pouch containing sacks of various colored sacred paints. On Tail-Feathers-Coming-over-the-Hill's left sat his medicine wife. I took my seat close to him on his right. Back of me, and all around the right side of the lodge from me, were a number of women. On the other side, opposite them, were the men and Chief Crow's medicine wife.

The ceremony opened with a prayer by Tail-Feathers-Coming-over-the-Hill, beseeching the gods to look with favor upon what was to be done. Then his wife arose and undid the fastenings of the medicines, and slowly, reverently, laid them on the couch between her and her husband. The opening song then began, the song of Po-no-kai´-ût-sin-in-ah (Elk-Tongue Chief). Oh, how I would like to inscribe that song here! Alice Fletcher says — and I know that she is right — that all Indian music is classical. But their tonal scale is far different from ours; we have not one musical instrument that can reproduce it. Never, never lived a white man who could sing these Blackfeet songs. As a boy, year after year, I tried to sing them, and always, failed; one has to take them in with his mother's milk in order to sing them correctly.

The song ended. The medicine woman, with a pair of sacred red-painted willow tongs, took a coal from the fire, placed it just in front of the sacred medicines, and dropped upon it a pinch of sweet grass. It burned, and, as the perfumed smoke arose, she and her man grasped handfuls of it and stroked their bodies, thus purifying themselves before handling the medicines. Then, all present joining in, they

OPENING OF THE ELK MEDICINE PIPE CERMONY

Left to right: The author; Tail-feathers-coming-over-the-hill; nis wife and the wife of Chief Crow, both medicine women; Chief Crow, medicine man, lifting the sacred roll o the medicine pipe; Medicine Weasel and Old Boy, singers sang the song of the real bear, the grizzly, while the medicine woman unfastened the outer wrapping of the medicine pipestem roll, which was bound with a strip of fur from a grizzly's back; and at the same time, in keeping with the time of the song, they made the sign for the bear, closed hands held upon each side of the head, representing its wide, rounding ears.

That song finished, the song of the buffalo began, the medicine man and the medicine woman clenching their hands and alternately putting one out before the other, representing the deliberate, ponderous tread of the animals as they traveled to and from the water. When that song was finished — and it was one to stir one's inmost soul — another wrapping, bound with buffalo fur, was undone, and all present besought the gods to have pity upon them.

Next came the fourth and last song, the song of the beaver, chief of water animals. And while it was being sung, the medicine woman unrolled the fourth and last wrapping, and the sacred medicine pipestem lay in sight of us all. At that all the women gave shrill cries of triumph, of victory; and all the medicine

The Elk Medicine Ceremony

men beginning a solemn chant to the Sun, Chief Crow advanced, received from the medicine wife of my old friend the sacred stem, and, extending the fan of feathers drooping from it, held it aloft and danced in time with the song to the doorway of the lodge and back again, and returned the stem to my friend, who reverently took and embraced it, and made a short prayer to the gods for the long life, good health, and happiness of us all, especially the little children of the tribe.

Next came my part in the ceremony. My old relative and friend felt around in his medicine pouch, got out a small sack of *a-san'*, the sacred red paint, and painted my face with it, at the same time beseeching the gods to give me, his brother, Ap-i-kun'i, long life, good health, and prosperity in all things. Then, having finished the painting and the prayer, he had his wife hand Chief Crow, his helper, the long red-painted wooden flute that goes with the medicine, and the latter, holding it aloft, danced with it almost to the doorway of the lodge, where he blew several soft, clear notes to the four corners of the earth, and then returned the flute to the woman. This was the Elk Medicine whistle, for imitating the weird call of that animal, and was used just now to call him, the ancient Elk god; to give me his favor, his pity. My friend then facing me, upon his knees began the thunder song, in which all joined, and, spreading his blanket-clad arms wide to represent the thunder bird wings, hovered before me, fanned me with his wings, the intent being to waft to me from him the sacred power. That over, all arose, and passing in line from the lodge, Chief Crow leading, danced through the camp and back again, and the ceremony ended.

I cannot begin to express how I felt all through the ceremony. I honored my people for their sincere faith, their reverence for their gods. And my thoughts went back to the time when they were the lords of these plains and mountains and knew not want. And not so very long ago they were a tribe of three thousand members, and now they number only eight or nine hundred, and those who have gone have mostly gone from want, from their susceptibility to disease because of lack of proper nourishment. Do you wonder that they feel bitterly toward the whites, who have

The Under-Water People

taken from them everything that made their life worth living?

Because we were to-day to embark upon the deep, dark waters of this lake, we yesterday had a little ceremony on the shore, beseeching the dread Under-Water People to have pity upon us and allow us to pass in safety over their domain. We had a little fire close to the water's edge, and having filled and lighted his pipe with a coal taken from it with his sacred red tongs, old Tail-Feathers-Coming-over-the-Hill smoked and made his prayers, at the same time casting into the water a little sack of his medicines as a sacrifice to the gods. It was a short ceremony, but satisfied even the most timid of the women: that all would be well with them during their voyage upon the lake.

And so, where we once had rude rafts of logs, lashed together with rawhide ropes, we this morning embarked in good boats and went all up the beautiful lake, past Red Eagle, and Little Chief, and Almost-a-Dog Mountains to the head of the lake, and looking back at the slope of Milk River Ridge saw the far-apart, enormous footprints of Heavy Runner, keeper of the buffalo.

Away back in ancient times, after Old Man had made buffalo and they had increased and covered the plains, they had great desire to wander westward and see what might be on the other side of the great mountains. The people — the Blackfeet — learning of this were greatly distressed. The far side of the mountains, away west and still westward to the shores of the Everywhere-Water, was the country of their enemies, many tribes of them, and should they get possession of the buffalo herds they would never let them return. What to do about it they had no idea, so they called upon Old Man for help.

Said he: "I made the buffalo to be plains animals, and here upon these plains they shall remain, and other-side tribes shall come to you and ask permission to kill a few of them now and then. So, don't worry. Go home now and attend to your affairs. All shall be well with you."

The people went home. They saw that the buffalo remained upon the plains in apparently as great numbers as ever. But some of

Old Man and the Buffalo

the hunters, to learn for sure if they were all
there, ascended the different passes of the
mountains and went down the other side for
some distance. There were no buffalo, not
even a few straggling bulls on the other side,
and they wondered how Old Man was keeping
them back. They soon learned. In a vision it
was revealed to an old medicine man that a
huge god, a man of enormous stature, was
patrolling the mountains from far south to the
everlasting snow of the north, and with a club
driving the buffalo back eastward as fast as
they came anywhere near the summit of the
range. And so it was that the other tribes —
those of the west — never got the buffalo.

On our way down the lake we passed the
beautiful Sun Camp and the chalets of the
Great Northern, perched upon the very spot
where Tail-Feathers-Coming-over-the-Hill and
I killed many a bighorn and goat in times gone
by. It was a favorite wintering place of the
animals, for the winds kept the steep mountain slope practically bare from snow. And
passing the mouth of the creek just above
the camp, I remembered that I had named it
after Thomas, and Colonel Robert, and the

Blackfeet Tales of Glacier National Park

Honorable Cecil Baring, of London, with whom I often hunted back in the eighties. In those days there were many bighorn and goats, and not a few grizzlies back in the basin at the head of the creek. And what amusing and sometimes exciting adventures we had with them! One morning we espied a "billy" goat on a ledge, and just as we saw him he moved to the back side of it and lay down, showing only an inch or two of the top of his back.

"Who will go up and rout him out, so that I can get a shot?" asked Colonel Baring, and Jack Bean, of Yellowstone fame, volunteered.

It was to be a steep, almost straight-up climb, so Jack laid down his rifle and started without encumbrance of any kind. At last he reached the shelf and stood up on it, and that "billy" came for him, head down! And Jack! Never have I seen a man come down a dangerous cliff so fast as he did! And he kept coming, falling, sliding, rolling, and then Colonel Baring fired and dropped the goat, and man and animal came the rest of the way to the foot of the place together! We had been too much concerned for the safety of our

The Story of Tobacco

friend to laugh, but when he at last stood up
and faced us, bloody, half-naked, but not
seriously hurt, we roared. But Jack never
even smiled: "Who would have thought that
a blankety-blank goat would go for a fellow!"
he exclaimed; and he went to the creek to
repair the damages to his person.

On this day, halting here and there along
the lake, we took some views of the scenery
and of our people, and at sunset were back
in our lodges. For some of us it is a last trip
over the old, familiar ground. My two old
friends, Tail-Feathers-Coming over-the-Hill
and Yellow Wolf, must soon go on to their
Shadow Land!

We were not too tired to-night for story-
telling, so, after the children had been put to
bed and all was quiet, Takes-Gun-Ahead gave
us the following, the story of tobacco, which
is called

NA-WAK´-O-SIS

"In that long ago time when the earth was
young, and people had not long been made,
a man threw some weeds upon a fire and

found that the odor, the smoke from their burning, was very pleasant. That night he had a vision and learned that this plant was strong medicine; that, when smoked in a pipe, which his vision explained to him how to make, it would be the right thing with which to offer prayers to the gods. He also taught the man the prayers and all the ceremony that went with the prayers; and told him how to plant the weeds, from the seeds on their tops, so that he could always have plenty of it.

"This man was very much pleased with what he had learned. He went to his three brother medicine men and told them all about it, and the four of them formed a society of themselves and no others, for the raising of the weed and its proper uses. But they were very stingy with this weed, which they named *na-wak'-o-sis,* and would only now and then give the people a leaf of it, although they raised large numbers of the stalks in every summer time.

"A young man named Lone Bull was very anxious to become a member of this medicine society, but because he had no medicines and knew not the rites of it, he was told

The Story of Tobacco

that he could not join it. At that time the camp of the people was close under Chief Mountain. He left it, with his woman and his pack dogs, and moved up to the river running out of the Inside Lakes, and there set up his lodge. Said he then to his woman: 'I have come up here to get medicines; in some way to find things that will enable me to become a raiser of *na-wak'-o-sis*. If I can do that, I shall be of great help to the people. Now, then, I am going to hunt and collect all the medicine skins I can find, and you stay at home, take care of the lodge, gather wood, and cook what meat we need. I shall bring in plenty of fat meat along with the skins.'

"The man went hunting every day, and the woman remained at home. One day, when the man was gone, she thought she heard singing; beautiful singing; but look where she would she could see no singers. She spoke to the man about it when he came home that evening, and made him feel uneasy: 'If you hear it again, look about more carefully,' he told her.

"She heard it the next day, and this time located it, right under the lodge. She went out to the bank of the river and looked at the bank: there, under the water, were beaver holes in it, and beaver cuttings upon the sandy bottom, and by that she knew that the lodge had been set up above a bank beaver's home, and that beavers were the singers. She went back to the lodge, lay down and put her ear to the ground, and could then hear them plainly, and was pleased. Their singing was so good that it was all that she could do to stop listening to them and begin cooking the evening meal.

"When Lone Bull came home that night she told him what she had learned, but he could hear nothing, although he put his ear close to the ground. Nor could he hear the singing the next evening, nor the next, although his woman could hear it plainly. So now the woman got her knife and cut a round hole in the ground, and Lone Bull laid his head in it and could then hear the singing. He told her to make the hole deeper; larger. She did so, and cut clear through the ground, and looking down he could see the beavers sitting in their home, singing beautiful songs, and dancing

The Story of Tobacco

strange and beautiful dances in time to them.

" 'Younger brothers, have pity on me!' he cried. 'Oh, my young brothers, teach me your medicine!'

"They looked up and saw him, and one answered: 'Close the hole that you have made, because the light disturbs us, and we will soon be with you.'

"They soon came in through the doorway, four fine-looking men, beautifully dressed. They had changed themselves from beavers to men. They took seats, and then one of them said to Lone Bull: 'Elder brother, what is it that you want of us? How can we help you?'

"Lone Bull told them what it was: his great desire to obtain *na-wak'-o-sis* and grow it for the people.

" 'We have that plant; like us it is from the water, a water medicine,' the beaver man told him; 'but before you can use it you have much to do, much to learn. You have to learn all our songs and prayers and dances and different ceremonies, and gather for the ceremonies a skin of every animal and bird that is of the water, one of each except the beavers, and of them there must be two. You know these animals and birds: otter, mink, muskrat; different kinds of ducks; the fish hawk, and all the other birds that get their food from the life of the water. Why? Because there are two great life-givers of this world: the sun, which gives heat, and water, that makes growth, and in our ceremonies the skins of these different animals are symbols of the water.'

" 'I shall collect them all, so teach me everything,' Lone Bull told them. And they began that very night.

"Day after day Lone Bull hunted the animals and birds, brought in their skins for his woman to cure, and night after night the beavers taught him their medicine, all the sacred prayers and dances and ceremonies of it. And at last he knew them all thoroughly.

"Then, one night, the beaver chief handed him some stalks of *na-wak'-o-sis,* the top stems all covered with little round seeds.

" 'These,' said he, 'are the children of the big-leaved plants; put them into the ground and they will grow and make other plants that bear children. And now, I must tell you just

The Story of Tobacco

how to plant: Gather a great, long, wide pile of old dry logs, dry brush and weeds, and set it afire. The heat from it will burn the ground, burn the sod, and make everything soft under it. Then, when the place has cooled, gather from around badger holes, squirrel holes, and wherever you can find it, plenty of the brown earth they have thrown out, and mix it with the burned black earth, so that it will not pack hard around the seeds, and keep them from coming up into the sunlight.

"'After you have taken all the seeds from the stems, you must put them in a sack and not touch them again with your hands. With an antelope horn you will make row after row of little holes all across the burned ground and only a hand apart, and with a buffalo-horn spoon drop a seed into each hole. When that is done, and it will require a long time, you and yours are to dance along each row of seed, singing the sacred songs, your feet lightly pressing down the ground over the seed. At the end of a row you must step across to the next row, and dance backward on that one, and forward on the next, and so on until the last row has been pressed down, and all your songs have been sung. Then you can go away from the place for a time. Return after one moon has passed, and you will find that the young plants have grown above the ground. Watch them, that insects do not destroy them. Give them water if the rains fail you. They will grow all summer, and fade with the ripening of the choke-cherries. Cut them then, care well for them, and you and your people will have a plenty for your winter smokes and ceremonies. There! I have told you all!'

"It was planting-time then. Lone Bull moved right up to the foot of the lower one of the Inside Lakes, and did everything that he had been told to do, his wife helping him in every way. People hunting from down Chief Mountain way came and saw his growing plants, and went home and told about them. The four medicine men just laughed. 'Ha!' They cried. 'He has no *na-wak´-o-sis*! He wanted to join us and we would not let him into our society. He but plants some useless weed.'

"But later on, just as their planting was getting ripe, a terrible hailstorm came along and

The Story of Tobacco

destroyed it all; every leaf was cut into fine pieces! They cried from grief! Then they said among themselves: *'Na-wak'-o-sis* we must have or our medicines will be without power. It may be that this Lone Bull really has the true plants: let us go up and see them.'

"They went, all the people with them, and saw that he had the sacred plants. The hailstorm had come nowhere near his place.

"Said they to him then: 'You have a big planting, and we will help you gather it, and you and we four will use it. You shall join us.'

"Lone Bull laughed long before he answered: 'I need no help from you. You shall each have a little of my planting for your own use, and you shall pay me well for it. The rest, excepting what I need, I shall give to the people, and hereafter they will always have all that they need of the plants.'

"And as he said that he would do, so he did, and the people gave him great praise and honor for it all, and he lived to great age. Kyi! Why not? He had the beaver — the water medicine! It is a powerful medicine to this day!"

Blackfeet Tales of Glacier National Park

A visitor in our camp this evening told a tale that ill pleases us. There is a tourist camp away up in Gun-Sight Pass, one of the most weirdly beautiful places in this whole country. There, the other day, an employee was putting up a table on which were painted arrows pointing to the different mountains, the name of each peak alongside its particular arrow.

A tourist standing near and watching the work suddenly exclaimed: "Why, over there is a peak that has no name. Can you not name it after me?"

"Certainly I can," the employee answered; and painted another arrow and inscribed beside it: "Lehnert Peak."

"And over there is a fine waterfall," the tourist said. "Will you please name it after my little daughter?"

"Sure!" said the man; and painted another arrow pointing to "Mary Frances Falls." Enough said!

V

IKS-I´-KWO-YI-A-TUK-TAI
(SWIFT CURRENT RIVER)

September 1.

WE moved up here the other day and made camp beside one of the most lovely lakes in all this Rocky Mountain country. In my time we called it Beaver Woman's Lake. It is now McDermott Lake. And what a name that is for one of Nature's gems! There are names for other lakes and peaks here just as bad as that, but we shall have nothing to say about them here. Only by an act of Congress can we get what we want done, and we have faith that within a reasonable time all these mountains and lakes and streams will bear the names of the great chiefs, medicine men, and warriors who traversed them before the white men came.

Some of us — all excepting our two old men and the women — have been riding over the different trails here, viewing the glaciers

ICEBERG LAKE

Immense bergs are continually dropping into it from the live glacier in background

The Jealous Women

and other places of interest, especially Iceberg Lake, where we saw a mass of ice as large as a house part from the glacier, splash down into the deep lake, and disappear, and after a time come up from the depths to the surface and create another commotion of the waters. It was a grand sight!

Tail-Feathers-Coming-over-the-Hill says that the lake with the unpronounceable white man's name — McDermott — should be called Jealous Women's Lake; that away back in the days of his youth, when the Kootenai Indians occasionally came to camp and hunt with the Blackfeet, he had a youthful friend of the mountain tribe who told him the following story: —

THE JEALOUS WOMEN

"In those days a young Kootenai, good of heart, a great hunter, and very brave, married twin sisters so alike that except for one thing they could not be told apart: one was a slow, the other a very fast, talker.

"In time the fast talker, named Marmot, became jealous of her sister, Camas, complaining all the time that she had to do the most of the lodge work, and that she was sure Camas said bad things about her to their man. Camas denied all this. 'I have never tried to place myself first with our man,' she said. 'We are twins; I love you dearly; our man's heart is so big that it holds us both in equal love. Now, be sensible! Cast out your bad thoughts for they are all wrong.'

"But Marmot persisted in believing that she was neglected; that her sister had all their man's affection; and she finally went to him with her complaint. He laughed. 'I love you just as much as I do your sister,' he said. 'Now, just think back and show me when and in what way I have shown that she is first with me!'

"Marmot sat down and thought. She thought a long time; remained silent. The man was very patient with her; he waited for her answer, but it did not come. At last he said: 'Well, you have thought a long time. Have you found one thing in which I gave her preference?'

"'No, I have n't, but all the same I believe that you love her best,' Marmot answered; and got up and went about her work.

"The man shook his head, made no answer

The Jealous Women

to that, and took up his weapons and went hunting down the river. At the time he was camped right here at this lake.

"The man had not gone far, moving slowly, carefully, through the timber and brush along the river, when he heard ahead a great splashing in the water, and, going closer, found that it was caused by two otters playing. They would chase each other in the water, then climb the bank and go as swift as arrows from a bow down a slide that they had made, and again chase and tumble each other over in the water. The man crept closer to the slide, an arrow in his bow, another in his hand, and, watching his chance, shot one of the players. He tried to get the other, but it dived and was gone before he could fit the other arrow to his bow: 'It is too bad that I did n't get the other. I would have liked a skin of these medicine skins for each of my women,' he said to himself.

"He took the otter home and handed it to Camas. 'That is yours,' he said. 'There were two of them. To-morrow, Marmot, I will get the other for you, and then you will each have a strong medicine skin.'

"Marmot said nothing, but looked cross.

"The man went hunting the next day but he could not find the other otter. He searched the river for many days and could not find one.

"And as the days passed, Marmot became more and more angry, and finally said to her sister: 'I have proof now that our man loves you best. He gave you the otter; he does not even try to get one for me. He hunts other animals every day, bighorn, goats, animals that live nowhere near the haunts of the otter.'

" 'Now, don't be foolish!' Camas answered. 'You know as well as I do that he has tried and tried to get the other otter for you. But at the same time he has to get meat for us: that is why he hunts the mountain animals.'

" 'Camas, the two of us can no longer live in this lodge,' cried Marmot. 'You are a bad woman! I hate you! I will fight you any way you say to see which of us shall be our man's one wife!'

"Then it was that, for the first time, Camas became angry: 'We have no weapons to fight with,' she answered, 'but I propose this: We will swim this lake across and back and across and back until one of us becomes tired and

The Jealous Women

drowns! Now, crazy woman, what do you say to that?'

" 'Come on! Come on!' Marmot cried, and ran to the shore and tore off her clothes. So did Camas, and the two rushed into the water and began their swim of hate. They crossed the lake; turned and came back; crossed again and started back, Camas well in the lead. She reached the shore in front of the lodge, dragged herself out on the shore, and turned. Her sister had gone down. There was not even a ripple on the still water. Marmot was drowned. Hardly knowing what she did, she put on her clothes and went into the lodge and cried and cried. The man came home. She was still crying. He asked her where Marmot was, and she cried all the harder, but at last told him all. Then the man cried. Together the two mourned for a long time, and searched the lake for the body of the lost one, and could not find it. So they moved away from the unhappy place and returned to the camp of their people, but it was a long time, a very long time, before they ceased mourning, and never again would they go anywhere near the lake. "Yes, this is the Lake of the Jealous Women!"

VI

Ni-na Us-tak-wi (Chief Mountain)

September 7.

WE came up here the other day to the foot of this great landmark of the country, and made camp beside a running spring in the edge of the timber. The mountain is most appropriately named. It is the outer one of an eastward projecting spur of the range, and is higher than any of the peaks behind it. A chief, a leader, should always be taller, more conspicuous in every way than his followers. This mountain gradually slopes up eastward from the one behind it to an altitude of 9056 feet, then drops in a sheer cliff several thousand feet to its steep slope running down to the plain. From several hundred miles to the north, and an equal distance to the south, and from the Bear Paw Mountains to the east, it can be plainly seen, grim, majestic, a veritable Chief of Mountains, and for that reason the Blackfeet so named it in the long ago.

Chief Mountain

The way to climb the mountain is by the long, narrow, and in places cut-walled ridge running up toward its summit from the west, and then one has but one cliff to surmount, the one almost at its crest. Only men and goats and bighorn can scale that cliff, but on the extreme summit lies an old buffalo skull, taken there by a Blackfoot in the long ago for a pillow rest while getting his medicine dream. There he fasted for days, and at last, in his weakened condition resulting from want of food and water, got his vision, his medicine which was to be his guardian through life. Who was it that came to him in his fasting dreams? Ancient Buffalo, perhaps; or, maybe, Morning Star. Whoever it was, he went staggering down the mountain and to camp, absolutely certain that he had found his guardian spirit, his medium for favor with the greatest god of all, the Sun, supreme ruler of this earth.

We are here again upon our own ground, the Blackfeet Reservation, and so once more have meat in camp, fat bighorn and fat mule deer, killed by our hunters. This was once a great wintering place for deer and elk, and, higher up, for bighorn. Some years ago a hunter, Na-mik´-ai-yi by name, trailed a band of elk around to the ridge behind the mountain and up its narrow way until they came to the foot of the cliff near the summit and could go no farther. There they turned back toward him and he fired one shot and dropped the leader. The others, afraid to try to dash past him, chose the one alternative: they rushed to the high cliff there on the north side of the ridge, and sprang from it, and were all killed by the fall, eighty head of them!

September 8.

Last night, after our feast of *ni-tap´-i-wak-sin* (real meat) we gathered in Yellow Wolf's lodge for a smoke and a talk, and our host gave us a little story that I must here set down, the story of

THE WISE MAN

"Here, under this mountain, the people were encamped and two of them were Wise Man[1] and his woman. He was so named because he was always finding out how to do useful things.

[1]Mo-kûk´-i In-ah.

220

The Wise Man

"Up to the time of this encampment the people had had nothing to wear but the plainest kind of garments, shirts, leggins, gowns, moccasins, all made of plain tanned leather of different kinds. Wise Man thought long about this, and finally said to his wife: 'Let us move away from camp for a time, and go farther into the mountains. I have a plan that I want to try by myself.'

"The next morning they packed their dogs and moved up to the foot of the Inside Lakes, crossed the outlet, and made camp. Wise Man then did some hunting, killed plenty of meat for his wife and the dogs, and began on his plan for making clothing more pleasing to the eye. He went up on the high ridge between lakes and Little River and dug an eagle trap. That is, he dug a pit somewhat longer and wider than his body, and quite deep, and killed a deer and laid it beside the pit, and slashed its body so that the liver protruded. He then got into the pit, covered the top of it with willow sticks and grass, and waited, hoping that eagles would see the deer and come to eat it. They did come; he could hear the heavy swish of their wings as they sailed down upon it; and as they were eating the liver he would cautiously reach up, grasp them by the legs, pull them down into the pit, and kneeling upon them crush out their life. In this way, one at a time, he caught many eagles, and took them home as he caught them, and took from their bodies the tail feathers, the fluffy plume feathers, and others that he thought would answer his purpose.

"They had a very rank, unpleasant odor, these feathers; so, when he thought that he had enough of them, he had his woman cover the floor of the lodge with a thick layer of sweet sage, upon which he carefully spread them. He then threw a quantity of sweetgrass upon the fire, and, running from the lodge, the two tightly closed it and kept the smoke inside. This last they did three or four times until the feathers lost their bad odor, and were perfumed with the pleasant odor of sweetgrass and sweet sage, both perfumes sacred to the gods, as they afterward learned.

"Winter was now come, and Wise Man began to hunt weasels, brown and common of appearance in summer, but white and beautiful in winter. This was more difficult work

The Wise Man

than trapping eagles, but by setting many snares he caught during the winter more than a hundred of them. He then made a head-dress of some of the eagle tail feathers, and suspended from it a number of weasel skins, and along the seams of his shirt and leggins tied a number of the weasel skins. He then put on the headdress and his ornamental clothes and stood up and asked his woman how he appeared in them.

" 'You seem to have become a different man,' she answered. 'You look very brave, very handsome. The clothes are beautiful.'

" 'They are of better appearance than they were,' he said, 'but I am not yet satisfied. Perhaps I can improve them; but first I have to do something for you.'

"Wise Man put away his new clothes, and in old ones hunted elk, taking from them their two tushes, and in the evening boring holes in the soft part. Having collected two hundred, he sewed them in rows on the breast and the back of his woman's new gown, and both saw that it was then a handsome gown.

"Said the woman: 'There! We are now complete; we have fine appearance. Let us go home and show the people what we have done.'

" 'No,' Wise Man answered; 'something is lacking, something that will make our clothes really beautiful. I have done all that I can without help, and now I shall ask the gods to show me what more to do.'

"Perhaps it was the gods that directed his footsteps the next day. As he was going through the timber he came upon the remains of a porcupine, its quills scattered all around upon the ground. He sat down, took up some and examined them, and the thought came to him that they could be dyed different colors and in some way sewed upon garments and make them of brighter hue. He took all that he could find, and killed several more porcupines, and carried home all the long quills to his woman and told her his plan.

"Said she, 'I know that the yellow moss that grows on pine trees will stain anything a yellow that will not fade, that cannot be washed off. Let us seek for other colors.'

"They sought a long time, finding a green color in a certain wood, a red in the juice of a plant, and then they dyed the quills the three

The Wise Man

colors. Meantime the woman had been trying different ways to fasten the quills to leather, and now, by flattening them, turning in the ends, and sewing them side by side with very fine sinew and with the finest of bone needles, she succeeded in making long bands of them of different designs in the various colors. She was a long, long time making them, but at last she made enough of the bands to sew onto the arms of Wise Man's shirt, and down his leggins, and upon the neck front-and-back of her gown. Each was so pleased with the appearance of the other then that they kissed and almost cried with joy. Early the following morning they packed up, crossed the river, and started for the camp, still here at Chief Mountain. As soon as they came in sight of it they stopped, put on their fine clothes, and then went on. The people saw them approaching, but not until they were right close to the camp were they recognized. Then what a crowd surrounded them, staring at their beautiful garments, asking questions without end, and as soon as they learned how this had all been done, they began at once to gather material for similar clothing. And Wise Man, of course, became a great man in the tribe, for to him was due the discovery of the way to make beautiful things."

September 9.

Although nothing has been said, we have not been so cheerful as usual for the past few days, for all have known that we must soon part and go our several ways. Tail-Feathers-Coming-over-the-Hill is a sick man, and Yellow Wolf but little better, so to-night we decided to break camp in the morning. To-morrow night each family will be at home on Cutbank, Willow Creek, Two Medicine, and Badger, all streams of the Reservation, and I shall be upon my way to the Always-Summer-Land.

Well, we have had a pleasant time these past two months, traveling and camping along our old trails, and yet the evenings around the lodge fires have not been of un-alloyed joy: all have been tinged with sad memories of other days; of deep regret that the old days — days when we had all this great country to ourselves — are gone for-ever. And so, to-night, after our quiet, last

The Wise Man

evening meal together, we had no story-telling, no passing of the pipe; none had the heart for it; and I am writing these last words by the light of a dying fire, true symbol of the passing of all things. And now, by its last, blue flicker, I write —

THE END

ABOUT THE AUTHOR

James Willard Schultz was born in Boonville, New York, in 1859. His upper-class family harbored hopes that he would follow in its footsteps into genteel society, but at a young age James amply demonstrated that his rebellious and adventurous predilections would lead him down a different path. Schoolrooms and book learning held little attraction for Schultz, who preferred the freedom of roaming the Adirondacks on hunting and camping trips under the tutelage of guides hired by his family. Thinking that James's fondness for the rough life in the woods and an interest in firearms presaged a military career, his family packed him off to Peekskill Military Academy on the Hudson in anticipation of his entering West Point.

An 1877 trip to his uncle's hotel in St. Louis, Missouri, however, altered his destiny. At the Planters Hotel in St. Louis, James encountered steamboat pilots, Indian fur traders, roustabouts, hide hunters, and other frontiersmen from the upper Missouri River country. They plied him with vivid stories of life among the Indians—which so fired his imagination that he soon booked passage to Fort Benton, Montana, on the steamboat *Far West*. Using letters of introduction, James fortuitously connected with Joseph Kipp, a fur trader with the Piegan Blackfeet. Working as fur trader, he ranged over northern Montana for five years with Kipp, enjoying a semi-nomadic life until the extermination of the bison in the early 1880s. Schultz married a Blackfeet woman named Fine Shield Woman, and the couple settled down upon a simple ranch on the Blackfeet reservation in 1885, raising livestock and guiding hunting parties into the mountains to the west (now known as Glacier National Park).

From 1885 until Fine Shield Woman's death in 1903, Schultz supplemented their income by writing articles for national newspapers and magazines. George Bird Grinnell, one of Schultz's hunting clients was the editor of *Forest and Stream*, was particularly impressed with Schultz's narration of frontier experiences, and a life-long friendship ensued between the two to their mutual benefit.

Not long after Fine shield Woman's death, Schultz became involved in a hunting violation scandal and chose to flee Montana. He eventually settled in California, where he worked first for an oil company and then a newspaper. During this unsettled period of his life, he penned his first—and perhaps finest—book length manuscript, *My Life as an Indian*. Its success begat a long writing career, for between 1907 and 1940 Schultz produced thirty-seven titles celebrating Indian life on the frontier. He died in 1947 at the age of eighty-eight.

Wonderful books about Glacier National Park

Place Names of Glacier National Park
Jack Holterman

Here are the unique stories behind 663 geographic names in
Glacier National Park and Waterton Lakes National Park. Readers
will be fascinated to learn the who, the how, and the why behind
the names of mountains, rivers, lakes, and locations.

Wildflowers of Glacier National Park
Shannon Fitzpatrick Kimball and Peter Lesica

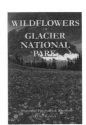

A user-friendly field guide to identifying more than 300 species
of wildflowers and plants, featuring superb color photos and
interesting facts about each plant.

Crown of the Continent:
The Last Great Wilderness of the Rocky Mountains

Ralph Waldt, Foreword by Ivan Doig
This multiple award-winning title describes the Crown of
the Continent ecosystem that includes Glacier National
Park. More than 150 spectacular color photos and superior
writing by naturalist Ralph Waldt, novelist Ivan Doig,
National Geographic writer Douglas Chadwick, and bear
biologist Dr. Charles Jonkel.
   "Stunning photographs and informed text make a strong
case for protecting the Crown of the Continent." – *Los Angeles Times*
"A magnificent book." – *Seattle Post-Intelligencer*

Blackfeet Indian Stories   George Bird Grinnell

Here are more great stories of the Blackfeet, recorded by the
famous conservationist and ethnologist who became a tribal
member in 1885.

Hiking with Grizzlies: Lessons Learned
Tim Rubbert

Unlike other books about hiking in grizzly
country, this book uses photographs of Rubbert's actual bear
encounters to dramatically illustrate how to react safely. Every
hiker will benefit from these first-hand, real-world lessons
drawn largely from experiences in Glacier National Park.

*Buy these books at your local bookstore or call Riverbend Publishing
toll-free 1-866-787-2363 or visit www.RiverbendPublishing.com.*